LILLIAN HELLMAN

THE CHILDREN'S HOUR

ALFRED · A · KNOPF

New York · 1936

PUBLISHED NOVEMBER 21, 1934
SECOND PRINTING, DECEMBER, 1934
THIRD PRINTING, FEBRUARY, 1935
FOURTH PRINTING, JANUARY, 1936

Manufactured in the United States of America

FOR

D. HAMMETT

WITH THANKS

THE CHILDREN'S HOUR *was produced and directed by Herman Shumlin at Maxine Elliott's Theatre, New York, on November 20, 1934. The settings were designed by Aline Bernstein.*

CAST

(In the order of their speech)

PEGGY ROGERS	*played by*	EUGENIA RAWLS
MRS. LILY MORTAR	" "	ALINE MC DERMOTT
EVELYN MUNN	" "	ELIZABETH SECKEL
HELEN BURTON	" "	LYNNE FISHER
LOIS FISHER	" "	JACQUELINE RUSLING
CATHERINE	" "	BARBARA LEEDS
ROSALIE WELLS	" "	BARBARA BEALS
MARY TILFORD	" "	FLORENCE MC GEE
KAREN WRIGHT	" "	KATHERINE EMERY
MARTHA DOBIE	" "	ANNE REVERE
DOCTOR JOSEPH CARDIN	" "	ROBERT KEITH
AGATHA	" "	EDMONIA NOLLEY
MRS. AMELIA TILFORD	" "	KATHERINE EMMET
A GROCERY BOY	" "	JACK TYLER

THE CHILDREN'S HOUR

∾ ∾

ACT I

Living-room of the Wright-Dobie School.
Late afternoon in April.

ACT II

Scene I. Living-room at Mrs. Tilford's. A few hours later.
Scene II. The same. Later that evening.

ACT III

The same as Act I. November.

ACT I

SCENE: A room in the Wright-Dobie School for girls,
a converted farm-house eighteen miles from the town
of Lancet. It is a comfortable, unpretentious room
used as an afternoon study-room and at all other times
as the living-room.
A large door Left Center faces the audience. There is a
single door Right. Against both back walls are book-
cases. A large desk is at Right; a table, two sofas, and
eight or ten chairs.
It is early in an afternoon in April.

AT RISE: MRS. LILY MORTAR *is sitting in a large chair*
Right Center, with her head back and her eyes closed.
She is a plump, florid woman of forty-five with obvi-
ously touched-up hair. Her clothes are too fancy for a
class-room.
Seven girls, from twelve to fourteen years old, are in-
formally grouped on chairs and sofa. Six of them are
sewing with no great amount of industry on pieces of
white material. One of the others, EVELYN MUNN, *is*
using her scissors to trim the hair of ROSALIE, *who sits,*
nervously, in front of her. She has ROSALIE's *head bent*
back at an awkward angle and is enjoying herself.
The eighth girl, PEGGY ROGERS, *is sitting in a higher*

3

chair than the others. She is reading aloud from a book. She is bored and she reads in a singsong, tired voice.

PEGGY [*reading*]: "It is twice blest; it blesseth him that gives and him that takes: 'tis mightiest in the mightiest; it becomes the throned monarch better than his crown; his sceptre shows the force of temporal power, the attribute to awe and majesty, wherein . . ." [MRS. MORTAR *suddenly opens her eyes and stares at the hair-cutting. The children make efforts to warn* EVELYN. PEGGY *raises her voice until she is shouting.*] "doth sit the dread and fear of kings; but mercy is above . . ."

MRS. MORTAR: Evelyn! What are you doing?

EVELYN [*inanely. She lisps*]: Uh—nothing, Mrs. Mortar.

MRS. MORTAR: You are certainly doing something. You are ruining the scissors, for one thing.

PEGGY [*loudly*]: "But mercy is above. It . . ."

MRS. MORTAR: Just a moment, Peggy. It is very unfortunate that you girls cannot sit quietly with your sewing and drink in the immortal words of the immortal bard. [*She sighs.*] Evelyn, go back to your sewing.

EVELYN: I can't get the hem thtraight. Honeth, I've been trying for three weekth, but I jutht can't do it.

MRS. MORTAR: Helen, please help Evelyn with the hem.

HELEN [*rises, holding up the garment* EVELYN *has been*

working on. It is soiled and shapeless, and so much has been cut off that it is now hardly large enough for a child of five. Giggling]: She can't ever wear *that*, Mrs. Mortar.

MRS. MORTAR [*vaguely*]: Well, try to do something with it. Make some handkerchiefs or something. Be clever about it. Women must learn these tricks. [*To* PEGGY.] Continue. "Mightiest in the mightiest."

PEGGY: " 'Tis mightiest in the mightiest; it becomes the throned monarch better than his crown; his sceptre— his sceptre shows the force of temporal power, the attribute to awe and majesty, wherein—"

LOIS [*from the back of the room chants softly and monotonously through the previous speech*]: Ferebam, ferebas, ferebat, ferebamus, ferebatis, fere, fere—

CATHERINE [*two seats away, the book propped in front of her*]: Fere*bant*.

LOIS: Ferebamus, ferebatis, fere*bant*.

MRS. MORTAR: Who's doing that?

PEGGY [*the noise ceases. She hurries on*]: Wherein doth sit the dread and fear of kings; but mercy is above this sceptred sway, it is enthroned in the hearts of kings, it is an attribute to God himself—

MRS. MORTAR [*sadly, reproachfully*]: Peggy, can't you imagine yourself as Portia? Can't you read the lines with some feeling, some pity? [*Dreamily.*] Pity. Ah! As Sir Henry said to me many's the time, pity makes the actress. Now, why can't *you* feel pity?

PEGGY: I guess I feel pity.

LOIS: Ferebamus, ferebatis, fere—fere—fere—

CATHERINE: Fere*bant*, stupid.

MRS. MORTAR: How many people in this room are talking? Peggy, read the line again. I'll give you the cue.

PEGGY: What's a cue?

MRS. MORTAR: A cue is a line or word given the actor or actress to remind them of their next speech.

HELEN [*softly*]: To remind *him* or *her*.

ROSALIE [*a fattish girl with glasses*]: Weren't you ever in the movies, Mrs. Mortar?

MRS. MORTAR: I had many offers, my dear. But the cinema is a shallow art. It has no—no— [*Vaguely.*] no fourth dimension. Now, Peggy, if you would only try to submerge yourself in this problem. You are pleading for the life of a man. [*She rises and there are faint sighs from the girls, who stare at her with blank, bored faces. She recites hammily, with gestures.*] "But mercy is above this sceptred sway; it is enthroned in the hearts of kings, it is an attribute to God himself; and earthly power doth then show likest God's when mercy seasons justice."

LOIS [*almost singing it*]: Utor, fruor, fungor, potior, and vescor take the dative.

CATHERINE: Take the *ablative*.

LOIS: Oh, dear. Utor, fruor, fung—

MRS. MORTAR [*to* LOIS, *with sarcasm*]: You have something to tell the class?

LOIS [*apologetically*]: We've got a Latin exam this afternoon.

MRS. MORTAR: And you intend to occupy the sewing and elocution hour learning what should have been learnt yesterday?

CATHERINE [*wearily*]: It takes her more than yesterday to learn it.

MRS. MORTAR: Well, I cannot allow you to interrupt us like this.

CATHERINE: But we're finished sewing.

LOIS [*admiringly*]: I bet you were good at Latin, Mrs. Mortar.

MRS. MORTAR [*conciliated*]: Long ago, my dear, long ago. Now, take your book over by the window and don't disturb our enjoyment of Shakespeare. [CATHERINE *and* LOIS *rise, go to window, stand mumbling and gesturing.*] Let us go back again. "It is an attribute of—" [*At this point the door opens far enough to let* MARY TILFORD, *clutching a slightly faded bunch of wild flowers, squeeze cautiously in. She is fourteen, neither pretty nor ugly. She is an undistinguished-looking girl, except for the sullenly dissatisfied expression on her face.*] "And earthly power doth then show likest God's when mercy seasons justice. We do pray for mercy, and that same prayer doth teach—"

PEGGY [*happily*]: You've skipped three lines.

MRS. MORTAR: In my entire career I've never missed a line.

PEGGY: But you did skip three lines. [*Goes to* MRS. MOR-TAR *with book.*] See?

MRS. MORTAR [*seeing* MARY *sidling along wall toward other end of the room, turns to her to avoid* PEGGY *and the book*]: Mary!

HELEN [*in whisper to* MARY]: You're going to catch it now.

MRS. MORTAR: Mary!

MARY: Yes, Mrs. Mortar?

MRS. MORTAR: This is a pretty time to be coming to your sewing class, I must say. Even if you have no interest in your work you might at least remember that you owe me a little courtesy. Courtesy is breeding. Breeding is an excellent thing. [*Turns to class.*] Always remember that.

ROSALIE: Please, Mrs. Mortar, can I write that down?

MRS. MORTAR: Certainly. Suppose you all write it down.

PEGGY: But we wrote it down last week.

[MARY *giggles.*]

MRS. MORTAR: Mary, I am still awaiting your explanation. Where have you been?

MARY: I took a walk.

MRS. MORTAR: So you took a walk. And may I ask, young lady, are we in the habit of taking walks when we should be at our classes?

MARY: I am sorry, Mrs. Mortar. I went to get you these flowers. I thought you would like them and I didn't know it would take so long to pick them.

MRS. MORTAR [*flattered*]: Well, well.

MARY [*almost in tears*]: You were telling us last week how much you liked flowers, and I thought that I would bring you some and—

MRS. MORTAR: That was very sweet of you, Mary; I always like thoughtfulness. But you must not allow anything to interfere with your classes. Now run along, dear, and get a vase and some water to put my flowers in. [MARY *turns, · sticks out her tongue at* HELEN, *says:* "A-a-a," *and exits Left.*] You may put that book away, Peggy. I am sure your family need never worry about your going on the stage.

PEGGY: I don't want to go on the stage. I want to be a lighthouse-keeper's wife.

MRS. MORTAR: Well, I certainly hope you won't read to him.

[*The laughter of the class pleases her.* PEGGY *sits down among the other girls, who are making a great show of doing nothing.* MRS. MORTAR *returns to her chair, puts her head back, closes her eyes.*]

CATHERINE: How much longer, O Cataline, are you going to abuse our patience? [*To* LOIS.] Now translate it, and for goodness' sakes try to get it right this time.

MRS. MORTAR [*for no reason*]: "One master passion in the breast, like Aaron's serpent, swallows all the rest."

[*She and* LOIS *are murmuring during* KAREN WRIGHT'S *entrance.* KAREN *is an attractive woman of twenty-eight, casually pleasant in manner, without sacrifice of warmth or dignity. She smiles at the girls, goes to the desk. With her entrance there is an immediate change in the manner of the girls: they are fond of her and they respect her. She gives* MORTAR, *whose quotation has reached her, an annoyed look.*]

LOIS: "Quo usque tandem a*bute*re. . . ."

KAREN [*automatically*]: "Abu*tere*." [*Opens drawer in desk.*] What's happened to your hair, Rosalie?

ROSALIE: It got cut, Miss Wright.

KAREN [*smiling*]: I can see that. A new style? Looks as though it has holes in it.

EVELYN [*giggling*]: I didn't mean to do it that bad, Mith Wright, but Rothalie'th got funny hair. I thaw a picture in the paper, and I wath trying to do it that way.

ROSALIE [*feels her hair, looks pathetically at* KAREN]: Oh, what shall I do, Miss Wright? [*Gesturing.*] It's long here, and it's short here and—

KAREN: Never mind. Come up to my room later and I'll see if I can fix it for you.

MRS. MORTAR: And hereafter we'll have no more hair-cutting.

KAREN: Helen, have you found your bracelet?

HELEN: No, I haven't, and I've looked everywhere.

KAREN: Have another look. It must be in your room somewhere.

[MARY *comes in Right, with her flowers in a vase. When she sees* KAREN, *she loses some of her assurance.*

KAREN *looks at the flowers in surprise.*]

MARY: Good afternoon, Miss Wright. [*Sits down, looks at* KAREN, *who is staring hard at the flowers.*]

KAREN: Hello, Mary.

MRS. MORTAR [*fluttering around*]: Peggy has been reading Portia for us.

[PEGGY *sighs.*]

KAREN [*smiling*]: Peggy doesn't like Portia?

MRS. MORTAR: I don't think she quite appreciates it, but—

KAREN [*patting* PEGGY *on the head*]: Well, I didn't either. I don't think I do yet. Where'd you get those flowers, Mary?

MRS. MORTAR: She picked them for me. [*Hurriedly.*] It made her a little late to class, but she heard me say I loved flowers, and she went to get them for me. [*With a sigh.*] The first wild flowers of the season.

KAREN: But not the very first, are they, Mary?

MARY: I don't know.

KAREN: Where did you get them?

MARY: Near Conway's cornfield, I think.

KAREN: It wasn't necessary to go so far. There was a bunch exactly like this in the garbage can this morning.

MRS. MORTAR [*after a second*]: Oh, I can't believe it! What a nasty thing to do! [*To* MARY.] And I suppose you have just as fine an excuse for being an hour late to breakfast this morning, and last week— [*To*

KAREN.] I haven't wanted to tell you these things before, but—

KAREN [*hurriedly, as a bell rings off stage*]: There's the bell.

LOIS [*walking toward door*]: Ad, ab, ante, in, de, inter, con, post, præ— [*Looks up at* KAREN.] I *can't* seem to remember the rest.

KAREN: Præ, pro, sub, super. Don't worry, Lois. You'll come out all right. [LOIS *smiles, exits.* MARY *attempts to make a quick exit.*] Wait a minute, Mary. [*Reluctantly* MARY *turns back as the girls file out.* KAREN *moves the small chairs, clearing the room as she talks.*] Mary, I've had the feeling—and I don't think I'm wrong—that the girls here were happy; that they liked Miss Dobie and me, that they liked the school. Do you think that's true?

MARY: Miss Wright, I have to get my Latin book.

KAREN: I thought it was true until you came here a year ago. I don't think you're very happy here, and I'd like to find out why. [*Looks at* MARY, *waits for an answer, gets none, shakes her head.*] Why, for example, do you find it necessary to lie to us so often?

MARY [*without looking up*]: I'm not lying. I went out walking and I saw the flowers and they looked pretty and I didn't know it was so late.

KAREN [*impatiently*]: Stop it, Mary! I'm not interested in hearing that foolish story again. I *know* you got the flowers out of the garbage can. What I do want to know is why you feel you have to lie out of it.

MARY [*beginning to whimper*]: I *did* pick the flowers near Conway's. You never believe me. You believe everybody but me. It's always like that. Everything I say you fuss at me about. Everything I do is wrong.

KAREN: You know that isn't true. [*Goes to* MARY, *puts her arm around her, waits until the sobbing has stopped.*] Look, Mary, look at me. [*Raises* MARY's *face with her hand.*] Let's try to understand each other. If you feel that you *have* to take a walk, or that you just *can't* come to class, or that you'd like to go into the village by yourself, come and tell me—I'll try and understand. [*Smiles.*] I don't say that I'll always agree that you should do exactly what you want to do, but I've had feelings like that, too—everybody has—and I won't be unreasonable about yours. But this way, this kind of lying you do, makes everything wrong.

MARY [*looking steadily at* KAREN]: I got the flowers near Conway's cornfield.

KAREN [*looks at* MARY, *sighs, moves back toward desk and stands there for a moment*]: Well, there doesn't seem to be any other way with you; you'll have to be punished. Take your recreation periods alone for the next two weeks. No horseback-riding and no hockey. Don't leave the school grounds for any reason whatsoever. Is that clear?

MARY [*carefully*]: Saturday, too?

KAREN: Yes.

MARY: But you said I could go to the boat-races.

KAREN: I'm sorry, but you can't go.

MARY: I'll tell my grandmother. I'll tell her how everybody treats me here and the way I get punished for every little thing I do. I'll tell her, I'll—

MRS. MORTAR: Why, I'd slap her hands!

KAREN [*turning back from door, ignoring* MRS. MORTAR's *speech. To* MARY]: Go upstairs, Mary.

MARY: I don't feel well.

KAREN [*wearily*]: Go upstairs now.

MARY: I've got a pain. I've had it all morning. It hurts right here [*pointing vaguely in the direction of her heart*]. Really it does.

KAREN: Ask Miss Dobie to give you some hot water and bicarbonate of soda.

MARY: It's a bad pain. I've never had it before.

KAREN: I don't think it can be very serious.

MARY: My heart! It's my heart! It's stopping or something. I can't breathe. [*She takes a long breath and falls awkwardly to the floor.*]

KAREN [*sighs, shakes her head, kneels beside* MARY. *To* MRS. MORTAR]: Ask Martha to phone Joe.

MRS. MORTAR [*going out*]: Do you think—? Heart trouble is very serious in a child.

[KAREN *picks* MARY *up from the floor and carries her off Right. After a moment* MARTHA DOBIE *enters Center.*

She is about the same age as KAREN. *She is a nervous,
high-strung woman.*]

KAREN [*enters Right*]: Did you get Joe?

MARTHA [*nodding*]: What happened to her? She was
perfectly well a few hours ago.

KAREN: She probably still is. I told her she couldn't go
to the boat-races and she had a heart attack.

MARTHA: Where is she?

KAREN: In there. Mortar's with her.

MARTHA: Anything really wrong with her?

KAREN: I doubt it. [*Sits down at desk and begins to mark
papers*]: She's a problem, that kid. Her latest trick
was kidding your aunt out of a sewing lesson with
those faded flowers we threw out. Then she threat-
ened to go to her grandmother with some tale about
being mistreated.

MARTHA: And, please God, Grandma would believe her
and take her away.

KAREN: Which would give the school a swell black eye.
But we ought to do something.

MARTHA: How about having a talk with Mrs. Tilford?

KAREN [*smiling*]: You want to do it? [MARTHA *shakes
her head.*] I hate to do it. She's been so nice to us.
[*Shrugging her shoulders*] Anyway, it wouldn't do
any good. She's too crazy about Mary to see her
faults very clearly—and the kid knows it.

MARTHA: How about asking Joe to say something to

her? She'd listen to him.

KAREN: That would be admitting that we can't do the job ourselves.

MARTHA: Well, we can't, and we might as well admit it. We've tried everything we can think of. She's had more attention than any other three kids put together. And we still haven't the faintest idea what goes on inside her head.

KAREN: She's a strange girl.

MARTHA: That's putting it mildly.

KAREN [*laughs*]: It's funny. We always talk about the child as if she were a grown woman.

MARTHA: It's not so funny. There's something the matter with the kid. That's been true ever since the first day she came. She causes trouble here; she's bad for the other girls. I don't know what it is—it's a feeling I've got that it's wrong somewhere—

KAREN: All right, all right, we'll talk it over with Joe. Now what about our other pet nuisance?

MARTHA [*laughs*]: My aunt the actress? What's she been up to now?

KAREN: Nothing unusual. Last night at dinner she was telling the girls about the time she lost her trunks in Butte, Montana, and how she gave her best performance of Rosalind during a hurricane. Today in the kitchen you could hear her on what Sir Henry said to her.

MARTHA: Wait until she does Hedda Gabler standing on

a chair. Sir Henry taught her to do it that way. He said it was a test of great acting.

KAREN: You must have had a gay childhood.

MARTHA [*bitterly*]: Oh, I did. I did, indeed. God, how I used to hate all that—

KAREN: Couldn't we get rid of her soon, Martha? I hate to make it hard on you, but she really ought not to be here.

MARTHA [*after a moment*]: I know.

KAREN: We can scrape up enough money to send her away. Let's do it.

MARTHA [*goes to her, affectionately pats her head*]: You've been very patient about it. I'm sorry and I'll talk to her today. It'll probably be a week or two before she can be ready to leave. Is that all right?

KAREN: Of course. [*Looks at her watch.*] Did you get Joe himself on the phone?

MARTHA: He was already on his way. Isn't he always on his way over here?

KAREN [*laughs*]: Well, I'm going to marry him some day, you know.

MARTHA [*looking at her*]: You haven't talked of marriage for a long time.

KAREN: I've talked of it with Joe.

MARTHA: Then you *are* thinking about it—soon?

KAREN: Perhaps when the term is over. By that time we ought to be out of debt, and the school should be paying for itself.

MARTHA [*nervously playing with a book on the table*]: Then we won't be taking our vacation together?

KAREN: Of course we will. The three of us.

MARTHA: I had been looking forward to some place by the lake—just you and me—the way we used to at college.

KAREN [*cheerfully*]: Well, now there will be three of us. That'll be fun, too.

MARTHA [*after a pause*]: Why haven't you told me this before?

KAREN: I'm not telling you anything we haven't talked about often.

MARTHA: But you're talking about it as *soon* now.

KAREN: I'm glad to be able to. I've been in love with Joe a long time. [MARTHA *crosses to window and stands looking out, her back to* KAREN. KAREN *finishes marking papers and rises.*] It's a big day for the school. Rosalie's finally put an "l" in could.

MARTHA [*in a dull, bitter tone, not turning from window*]: You really *are* going to leave, aren't you?

KAREN: I'm not going to leave, and you know it. Why do you say things like that? We agreed a long time ago that my marriage wasn't going to make any difference to the school.

MARTHA: But it will. You know it will. It can't help it.

KAREN: That's nonsense. Joe doesn't want me to give up here.

MARTHA [*turning from window*]: I don't understand

you. It's been so damned hard building this thing up, slaving and going without things to make ends meet— think of having a winter coat without holes in the lining again!—and now when we're getting on our feet, you're all ready to let it go to hell.

KAREN: This is a silly argument, Martha. Let's quit it. You haven't listened to a word I've said. I'm not getting married tomorrow, and when I do, it's not going to interfere with my work here. You're making something out of nothing.

MARTHA: It's going to be hard going on alone afterwards.

KAREN: For God's sake, do you expect me to give up my marriage?

MARTHA: I don't mean that, but it's so—

[Door Center opens and DOCTOR JOSEPH CARDIN comes in. He is a large, pleasant-looking, carelessly dressed man of about thirty-five.]

CARDIN: Hello, darling. Hi, Martha. What's the best news?

MARTHA: Hello, Joe.

KAREN: We tried to get you on the phone. Come in and look at your little cousin.

CARDIN: Sure. What's the matter with her now? I stopped at Vernie's on the way over to look at that little black bull he bought. He's a baby! There's going to be plenty of good breeding done in these hills.

KAREN: You'd better come and see her. She says she has

a pain in her heart. [*Goes out Right.*]

CARDIN [*stopping to light a cigarette*]: Our little Mary pops up in every day's dispatches.

MARTHA [*impatiently*]: Go and see her. Heart attacks are nothing to play with.

CARDIN [*looks at her*]: Never played with one in my life. [*Exits Right.*]

[MARTHA *walks around room and finally goes to stare out window.*]

[MRS. MORTAR *enters Right.*]

MRS. MORTAR: *I* was asked to leave the room. [MARTHA *pays no attention.*] It seems that I'm not wanted in the room during the examination.

MARTHA [*over her shoulder*]: What difference does it make?

MRS. MORTAR: What difference does it make? Why, it was a deliberate snub.

MARTHA: There's very little pleasure in watching a man use a stethoscope.

MRS. MORTAR: Isn't it natural that the child should have me with her? Isn't it natural that an older woman should be present? [*No answer.*] Very well, if you are so thick-skinned that you don't resent these things—

MARTHA: What are you talking about? Why, in the name of heaven, should *you* be with her?

MRS. MORTAR: It—it's customary for an older woman to be present during an examination.

MARTHA [*laughs*]: Tell that to Joe. Maybe he'll give you a job as duenna for his office.

MRS. MORTAR [*reminiscently*]: It was I who saved Delia Lampert's life the time she had that heart attack in Buffalo. We almost lost her that time. Poor Delia! We went over to London together. She married Robert Laffonne. Not seven months later he left her and ran away with Eve Cloun, who was playing the Infant Phenomenon in Birmingham—

MARTHA: Console yourself. If you've seen one heart attack, you've seen them all.

MRS. MORTAR: So you don't resent your aunt being snubbed and humiliated?

MARTHA: Oh, Aunt Lily!

MRS. MORTAR: Karen is consistently rude to me, and you know it.

MARTHA: I know that she is very polite to you, and— what's more important—very patient.

MRS. MORTAR: Patient with me? *I*, who have worked my fingers to the bone!

MARTHA: Don't tell yourself that too often, Aunt Lily; you'll come to believe it.

MRS. MORTAR: I *know* it's true. Where could you have gotten a woman of my reputation to give these children voice lessons, elocution lessons? Patient with me! Here I've donated my services—

MARTHA: I was under the impression you were being paid.

MRS. MORTAR: That small thing? I used to earn twice that for one performance.

MARTHA: The gilded days. It was very extravagant of them to pay you so much. [*Suddenly tired of the whole thing.*] You're not very happy here, are you, Aunt Lily?

MRS. MORTAR: Satisfied enough, I guess, for a poor relation.

MARTHA [*makes a motion of distaste*]: But you don't like the school or the farm or—

MRS. MORTAR: I told you at the beginning you shouldn't have bought a place like this. Burying yourself on a farm! You'll regret it.

MARTHA: We like it here. [*After a moment.*] Aunt Lily, you've talked about London for a long time. Would you like to go over?

MRS. MORTAR [*with a sigh*]: It's been twenty years, and I shall never live to see it again.

MARTHA: Well, you can go any time you like. We can spare the money now, and it will do you a lot of good. You pick out the boat you want and I'll get the passage. [*She has been talking rapidly, anxious to end the whole thing.*] Now that's all fixed. You'll have a grand time seeing all your old friends, and if you live sensibly I ought to be able to let you have enough to get along on. [*She begins to gather books, notebooks, and pencils.*]

MRS. MORTAR [*slowly*]: So you want me to leave?

MARTHA: That's not the way to put it. You've wanted to go ever since I can remember.

MRS. MORTAR: You're trying to get rid of me.

MARTHA: That's it. We don't want you around when we dig up the buried treasure.

MRS. MORTAR: So? You're turning me out? At my age! Nice, grateful girl you are.

MARTHA: Oh, my God, how can anybody deal with you? You're going where you want to go, and we'll be better off alone. That suits everybody. You complain about the farm, you complain about the school, you complain about Karen, and now you have what you want and you're still looking for something to complain about.

MRS. MORTAR [*with dignity*]: Please do not raise your voice.

MARTHA: You ought to be glad I don't do worse.

MRS. MORTAR: I absolutely refuse to be shipped off three thousand miles away. I'm not going to England. I shall go back to the stage. I'll write to my agents tomorrow, and as soon as they have something good for me—

MARTHA: The truth is I'd like you to leave soon. The three of us can't live together, and it doesn't make any difference whose fault it is.

MRS. MORTAR: You wish me to go tonight?

MARTHA: Don't act, Aunt Lily. Go as soon as you've found a place you like. I'll put the money in the bank for you tomorrow.

MRS. MORTAR: You think I'd take your money? I'd rather scrub floors first.

MARTHA: I imagine you'll change your mind.

MRS. MORTAR: I should have known by this time that the wise thing is to stay out of your way when *he's* in the house.

MARTHA: What are you talking about now?

MRS. MORTAR: Never mind. I should have known better. You always take your spite out on me.

MARTHA: Spite? [*Impatiently.*] Oh, don't let's have any more of this today. I'm tired. I've been working since six o'clock this morning.

MRS. MORTAR: Any day that he's in the house is a bad day.

MARTHA: When *who* is in the house?

MRS. MORTAR: Don't think you're fooling me, young lady. I wasn't born yesterday.

MARTHA: Aunt Lily, the amount of disconnected unpleasantness that goes on in your head could keep a psychologist busy for years. Now go take your nap.

MRS. MORTAR: I know what I know. Every time that man comes into this house, you have a fit. It seems like you just can't stand the idea of them being together. God knows what you'll do when they get married. You're jealous of him, that's what it is.

MARTHA [*her voice is tense and the previous attitude of good-natured irritation is gone*]: I'm very fond of Joe, and you know it.

MRS. MORTAR: You're fonder of Karen, and I know that. And it's unnatural, just as unnatural as it can be. You don't like their being together. You were always like that even as a child. If you had a little girl friend, you always got mad when she liked anybody else. Well, you'd better get a beau of your own now—a woman of your age.

MARTHA: The sooner you get out of here, the better. Your vulgarities are making me sick and I won't stand for them any longer. I want you to leave—

[*At this point there is a sound outside the large doors Center.* MARTHA *breaks off, angry and ashamed. After a moment she crosses to the door and opens it.* EVELYN *and* PEGGY *are to be seen on the staircase. For a second she stands still as they stop and look at her. Then, afraid that her anger with her aunt will color anything she might say to the children, she crosses the room again and stands with her back to them.*]

MARTHA: What were you doing outside the door?

EVELYN [*hurriedly*]: We were going upthtairth, Mith Dobie.

PEGGY: We came down to see how Mary was.

MARTHA: And you stopped long enough to see how we were. Did you deliberately listen?

PEGGY: We didn't mean to. We heard voices and we

couldn't help—

MRS. MORTAR [*fake social tone*]: Eavesdropping is something nice young ladies just don't do.

MARTHA [*turning to face the children*]: Go upstairs now. We'll talk about this later. [*Slowly shuts door as they begin to climb the stairs.*]

MRS. MORTAR: You mean to say you're not going to do anything about that? [*No answer. She laughs nastily.*] That's the trouble with these new-fangled notions of discipline and—

MARTHA [*thoughtfully*]: You know, it's really bad having you around children.

MRS. MORTAR: What exactly does that mean?

MARTHA: It means that I don't like them hearing the things you say. Oh, I'll "do something about it," but the truth is that this is their home, and things shouldn't be said in it that they can't hear. When you're at your best, you're not for tender ears.

MRS. MORTAR: So now it's my fault, is it? Just as I said, whenever he's in the house you think you can take it out on me. You've got to have some way to let out steam and—

[*Door opens Right and* CARDIN *comes in.*]

MARTHA: How is Mary?

[MRS. MORTAR, *head in air, gives* MARTHA *a malicious half-smile and makes what she thinks is majestic exit Center.*]

MRS. MORTAR: Good day, Joseph.

CARDIN: What's the matter with the Duchess? [*Nods at door Center.*]

MARTHA: Just keeping her hand in, in case Sir Henry's watching her from above. What about Mary?

CARDIN: Nothing. Absolutely nothing.

MARTHA [*sighs*]: I thought so.

CARDIN: I could have managed a better faint than that when I was six years old.

MARTHA: Nothing the matter with her at all, then?

CARDIN [*laughs*]: No, ma'am, not a thing. Just a little something she thought up.

MARTHA: But it's such a silly thing to do. She knew we'd have you in. [*Sighs.*] Maybe she's not so bright. Any idiots in your family, Joe? Any inbreeding?

CARDIN: Don't blame her on me. It's another side of the family. [*Laughs.*] You can look at Aunt Amelia and tell: old New England stock; never married out of Boston; still thinks honor is honor and dinner's at eight thirty. Yes, ma'am, we're a proud old breed.

MARTHA: The Jukes were an old family, too. Look, Joe, have you any idea what is the matter with Mary? I mean, has she always been like this?

CARDIN: She's always been a honey. Aunt Amelia's spoiling hasn't helped any, either.

MARTHA: We're reaching the end of our rope with her. This kind of thing—

CARDIN [*looking at her*]: Aren't you taking this too seriously?

MARTHA [*after a second*]: I guess I am. But you stay around kids long enough and you won't know what to take seriously, either. But I do think somebody ought to talk to Mrs. Tilford about her.

CARDIN: You wouldn't be meaning me now, would you, Miss Dobie?

MARTHA: Well, Karen and I were talking about it this afternoon and—

CARDIN: Listen, friend, I'm marrying Karen, but I'm not writing Mary Tilford in the contract. [MARTHA *moves slightly.* CARDIN *takes her by the shoulders and turns her around to face him again. His face is grave, his voice gentle.*] Forget Mary for a minute. You and I have got something to fight about. Every time anything's said about marrying—about Karen marrying me—you—[*She winces.*] There it is. I'm fond of you. I always thought you liked me. What is it? I know how fond you are of Karen, but our marriage oughtn't to make a great deal of difference—

MARTHA [*pushing his hands from her shoulders*]: God damn you. I wish— [*She puts her face in her hands.* CARDIN *watches her in silence, mechanically lighting a cigarette. When she takes her hands from her face, she holds them out to him. Contritely.*] Joe, please, I'm sorry. I'm a fool, a nasty, bitter—

CARDIN [*takes her hands in one of his, patting them with his other hand*]: Aw, shut up. [*He puts an arm around her, and she leans her head against his lapel.*

They are standing like that when KAREN *comes in Right.*]

MARTHA [*to* KAREN, *as she wipes her eyes*]: Your friend's got a nice shoulder to weep on.

KAREN: He's an admirable man in every way. Well, the angel child is now putting her clothes back on.

MARTHA: The angel child's influence is abroad even while she's unconscious. Her room-mates were busy listening at the door while Aunt Lily and I were yelling at each other.

KAREN: We'll have to move those girls away from one another.

[*A bell rings from the rear of the house.*]

MARTHA: That's my class. I'll send Peggy and Evelyn down. You talk to them.

KAREN: All right. [*As* MARTHA *exits Center,* KAREN *goes toward door Right. As she passes* CARDIN *she kisses him.*] Mary!

[MARY *opens door, comes in, stands buttoning the neck of her dress.*]

CARDIN [*to* MARY]: How's it feel to be back from the grave?

MARY: My heart hurts.

CARDIN [*laughing. To* KAREN]: Science has failed. Try a hairbrush.

MARY: It's *my* heart, and it hurts.

KAREN: Sit down.

MARY: I want to see my grandmother. I want to—

[EVELYN *and* PEGGY *timidly enter Center.*]

KAREN: Sit down, girls, I want to talk to you.

PEGGY: We're awfully sorry, really. We just didn't think and—

KAREN: I'm sorry too, Peggy. [*Thoughtfully.*] You and Evelyn never used to do things like this. We'll have to separate you three.

EVELYN: Ah, Mith Wright, we've been together almotht a year.

KAREN: It was evidently too long. Now don't let's talk about it. Peggy, you will move into Lois's room, and Lois will move in with Evelyn. Mary will go in with Rosalie.

MARY: Rosalie hates me.

KAREN: That's a very stupid thing to say. I can't imagine Rosalie hating anyone.

MARY [*starting to cry*]: And it's all because I had a pain. If anybody else was sick they'd be put to bed and petted. You're always mean to me. I get blamed and punished for everything. [*To* CARDIN.] I do, Cousin Joe. All the time for everything.

[MARY *by now is crying violently and as* KAREN *half moves toward her,* CARDIN, *who has been frowning, picks* MARY *up and puts her down on the couch.*]

CARDIN: You've been unpleasant enough to Miss Wright. Lie here until you've stopped working yourself into a fit. [*Picks up his hat and bag, smiles at* KAREN.] I've got to go now. She's not going to hurt herself crying. The next time she faints, I'd wait until she got tired lying on the floor. [*Passing* MARY, *he pats her head. She jerks away from him.*]

KAREN: Wait a minute. I'll walk to the car with you. [*To girls.*] Go up now and move your things. Tell Lois to get her stuff ready.

[*She and* CARDIN *exit Center. A second after the door is closed,* MARY *springs up and throws a cushion at the door.*]

EVELYN: Don't do that. She'll hear you.

MARY: Who cares if she does? [*Kicks table.*] And she can hear that, too.

[*Small ornament falls off table and breaks on floor.* EVELYN *and* PEGGY *gasp, and* MARY's *bravado disappears for a moment.*]

EVELYN [*frightened*]: Now what are you going to do?

PEGGY [*stooping down in a vain effort to pick up the pieces*]: You'll get the devil now. Dr. Cardin gave it to Miss Wright. I guess it was kind of a lover's gift. People get awfully angry about a lover's gift.

MARY: Oh, leave it alone. She'll never know we did it.

PEGGY: *We* didn't do it. You did it yourself.

MARY: And what will you do if I say *we* did do it? [*Laughs.*] Never mind, I'll think of something else. The wind could've knocked it over.

EVELYN: Yeh. She'th going to believe that one.

MARY: Oh, stop worrying about it. I'll get out of it.

EVELYN: Did you really have a pain?

MARY: I fainted, didn't I?

PEGGY: I wish I could faint sometimes. I've never even worn glasses, like Rosalie.

MARY: A lot it'll get you to faint.

EVELYN: What did Mith Wright do to you when the clath left?

MARY: Told me I couldn't go to the boat-races.

EVELYN: Whew!

PEGGY: But we'll remember everything that happens and we'll give you all the souvenirs and things.

MARY: I won't let you go if I can't go. But I'll find some way to go. What were *you* doing?

PEGGY: I guess we shouldn't have done it, really. We came down to see what was happening to you, but the doors were closed and we could hear Miss Dobie and Mortar having an awful row. Then Miss Dobie opens the door and there we were.

MARY: And a lot of crawling and crying you both did too, I bet.

EVELYN: We were thort of thorry about lithening. I gueth it wathn't—

MARY: Ah, you're always sorry about everything. What were they saying?

PEGGY: What was who saying?

MARY: Dobie and Mortar, silly.

PEGGY [*evasively*]: Just talking, I guess.

EVELYN: Fighting, you mean.

MARY: About what?

EVELYN: Well, they were talking about Mortar going away to England and—

PEGGY: You know, it really wasn't very nice to've listened, and I think it's worse to tell.

MARY: You do, do you? You just don't tell me and see what happens.

[PEGGY *sighs.*]

EVELYN: Mortar got awful thore at that and thaid they juth wanted to get rid of her, and then they thtarted talking about Dr. Cardin.

MARY: What about him?

PEGGY: We'd better get started moving; Miss Wright will be back first thing we know.

MARY [*fiercely*]: Shut up! Go on, Evelyn.

EVELYN: They're going to be married.

MARY: Everybody knows that.

PEGGY: But everybody doesn't know that Miss Dobie doesn't want them to get married. How do you like that?

[*The door opens and* ROSALIE WELLS *sticks her head in.*]

ROSALIE: I have a class soon. If you're going to move your things—

MARY: Close that door, you idiot. [ROSALIE *closes door, stands near it.*] What do you want?

ROSALIE: I'm trying to tell you. If you're going to move your things—not that I want you in with me—you'd better start right now. Miss Wright's coming in a minute.

MARY: Who cares if she is?

ROSALIE [*starts for door*]: I'm just telling you for your own good.

PEGGY [*getting up*]: We're coming.

MARY: No. Let Rosalie move our things.

ROSALIE: You crazy?

PEGGY [*nervously*]: It's all right. Evelyn and I'll get your things. Come on, Evelyn.

MARY: Trying to get out of telling me, huh? Well, you won't get out of it that way. Sit down and stop being such a sissy. Rosalie, you go on up and move my things and don't say a word about our being down here.

ROSALIE: And who was your French maid yesterday, Mary Tilford?

MARY [*laughing*]: You'll do for today. Now go on, Rosalie, and fix our things.

ROSALIE: You crazy?

MARY: And the next time we go into town, I'll let you wear my gold locket .and buckle. You'll like that, won't you, Rosalie?

ROSALIE [*draws back, moves her hands nervously*]: I don't know what you're talking about.

MARY: Oh, I'm not talking about anything in particular. You just run along now and remind me the next time to get my buckle and locket for you.

ROSALIE [*stares at her a moment*]: All right, I'll do it this time, but just 'cause I got a good disposition. But

don't think you're going to boss me around, Mary
Tilford.

MARY [*smiling*]: No, indeed. [ROSALIE *starts for door.*]
And get the things done neatly, Rosalie. Don't muss
my white linen bloomers—

[*The door slams as* MARY *laughs.*]

EVELYN: Now what do you think of that? What made
her tho agreeable?

MARY: Oh, a little secret we got. Go on, now, what else
did they say?

PEGGY: Well, Mortar said that Dobie was jealous of
them, and that she was like that when she was a little
girl, and that she'd better get herself a beau of her
own because it was unnatural, and that she never
wanted anybody to like Miss Wright, and that was
unnatural. Boy! Did Miss Dobie get sore at that!

EVELYN: Then we didn't hear any more. Peggy dropped
a book.

MARY: What'd she mean Dobie was jealous?

PEGGY: What's unnatural?

EVELYN: Un for not. Not natural.

PEGGY: It's funny, because everybody gets married.

MARY: A lot of people don't—they're too ugly.

PEGGY [*jumps up, claps her hand to her mouth*]: Oh,
my God! Rosalie'll find that copy of *Mademoiselle
de Maupin*. She'll blab like the dickens.

MARY: Ah, she won't say a word.

EVELYN: Who getth the book when we move?

MARY: You can have it. That's what I was doing this morning—finishing it. There's one part in it—

PEGGY: What part?

[MARY *laughs.*]

EVELYN: Well, what wath it?

MARY: Wait until you read it.

EVELYN: Don't forget to give it to me.

PEGGY: It's a shame about being moved. I've got to go in with Helen, and she blows her nose all night. Lois told me.

MARY: It was a dirty trick making us move. She just wants to see how much fun she can take away from me. She hates me.

PEGGY: No, she doesn't, Mary. She treats you just like the rest of us—almost better.

MARY: That's right, stick up for your crush. Take her side against mine.

PEGGY: I didn't mean it that way.

EVELYN [*looks at her watch*]: We'd better get up-thtairth.

MARY: I'm not going.

PEGGY: Rosalie isn't so bad.

EVELYN: What you going to do about the vathe?

MARY: I don't care about Rosalie and I don't care about the vase. I'm not going to be here.

EVELYN *and* PEGGY [*together*]: Not going to be here! What do you mean?

MARY [*calmly*]: I'm going home.

PEGGY: Oh, Mary—

EVELYN: You can't do that.

MARY: Can't I? You just watch. [*Begins to walk around the room.*] I'm not staying here. I'm going home and tell Grandma I'm not staying any more. [*Smiles to herself.*] I'll tell her I'm not happy. They're scared of Grandma—she helped 'em when they first started, you know—and when she tells 'em something, believe me, they'll sit up and listen. They can't get away with treating me like this, and they don't have to think they can.

PEGGY [*appalled*]: You just going to walk out like that?

EVELYN: What you going to tell your grandmother?

MARY: Oh, who cares? I'll think of something to tell her. I can always do it better on the spur of the moment.

PEGGY: She'll send you right back.

MARY: You let me worry about that. Grandma's very fond of me, on account my father was her favorite son. I can manage *her* all right.

PEGGY: I don't think you ought to go, really, Mary. It's just going to make an awful lot of trouble.

EVELYN: What'th going to happen about the vathe?

MARY: Say I did it—it doesn't make a bit of difference any more to me. Now listen, you two got to help. They won't miss me before dinner if you make Rosalie shut the door and keep it shut. Now, I'll go through the field to French's, and then I can get the bus to Homestead.

EVELYN: How you going to get to the thtreet-car?

MARY: Taxi, idiot.

PEGGY: How are you going to get out of here in the first place?

MARY: I'm going to walk out. You know where the front door is, or are you too dumb even for that? Well, I'm going right out that front door.

EVELYN: Gee, I wouldn't have the nerve.

MARY: Of course you wouldn't. You'd let 'em do anything to you they want. Well, they can't do it to me. Who's got any money?

EVELYN: Not me. Not a thent.

MARY: I've got to have at least a dollar for the taxi and a dime for the bus.

EVELYN: And where you going to find it?

PEGGY: See? Why don't you just wait until your allowance comes Monday, and then you can go any place you want. Maybe by that time—

MARY: I'm going today. *Now.*

EVELYN: You can't *walk* to Lanthet.

MARY [*goes to* PEGGY]: You've got money. You've got two dollars and twenty-five cents.

PEGGY: I—I—

MARY: Go get it for me.

PEGGY: No! No! I won't get it for you.

EVELYN: You can't have *that* money, Mary—

MARY: Get it for me.

PEGGY [*cringes, her voice is scared*]: I won't. I won't. Mamma doesn't send me much allowance—not half as much as the rest of you get—I saved this so long— you took it from me last time—

EVELYN: Ah, she wantth that bithycle tho bad.

PEGGY: I haven't gone to the movies, I haven't had any candy, I haven't had anything the rest of you get all the time. It took me so long to save that and I—

MARY: Go upstairs and get me the money.

PEGGY [*hysterically, backing away from her*]: I won't. I won't. I won't.

[MARY *makes a sudden move for her, grabs her left arm, and jerks it back, hard and expertly.* PEGGY *screams softly.* EVELYN *tries to take* MARY's *arm away. Without releasing her hold on* PEGGY, MARY *slaps* EVELYN's *face.* EVELYN *begins to cry.*]

MARY: Just say when you've had enough.

PEGGY [*softly, stiflingly*]: All—all right—I'll get it.

[MARY *smiles, nods her head as the Curtain falls.*]

ACT II

SCENE: *Living-room at* MRS. TILFORD'S. *It is a formal room, without being cold or elegant. The furniture is old, but excellent. The exit to the hall is Left; glass doors Right lead to a dining-room that cannot be seen.*

AT RISE: *Stage is empty. Voices are heard in the hall.*

AGATHA [*off-stage*]: What are *you* doing here? Well, come on in—don't stand there gaping at me. Have they given you a holiday or did you just decide you'd get a better dinner here? [AGATHA *enters Left, followed by* MARY. AGATHA *is a sharp-faced maid, no longer young, with a querulous voice.*] Can't you even say hello?

MARY: Hello, Agatha. You didn't give me a chance. Where's Grandma?

AGATHA: Why aren't you in school? Look at your face and clothes. Where have you been?

MARY: I got a little dirty coming home. I walked part of the way through the woods.

AGATHA: Why didn't you put on your middy blouse and your old brown coat?

MARY: Oh, stop asking me questions. Where's Grandma?

43

AGATHA: Where ought any clean person be at this time of day? She's taking a bath.

MARY: Is anybody coming for dinner?

AGATHA: She didn't say anything about you coming.

MARY: How could she, stupid? She didn't know.

AGATHA: Then what are you doing here?

MARY: Leave me alone. I don't feel well.

AGATHA: Why don't you feel well? Who ever heard of a person going for a walk in the woods when they didn't feel well?

MARY: Oh, leave me alone. I came home because I was sick.

AGATHA: You look all right.

MARY: But I don't feel all right. [*Whining.*] I can't even come home without everybody nagging at me.

AGATHA: Don't think you're fooling me, young lady. You might pull the wool over some people's eyes, but—I bet you've been up to something again. [*Stares suspiciously at* MARY, *who says nothing.*] Well, you wait right here till I tell your grandmother. And if you feel so sick, you certainly won't want any dinner. A good dose of rhubarb and soda will fix you up. [*Exits Left.*]

[MARY *makes a face in the direction* AGATHA *has gone and stops sniffling. She looks nervously around the room, then goes to a low mirror and tries several experiments with her face in an attempt to make it look sick and haggard.*]

[MRS. TILFORD, *followed by* AGATHA, *enters Left.* MRS. TILFORD *is a large, dignified woman in her sixties, with a pleasant, strong face.*]

AGATHA [*to* MRS. TILFORD, *as she follows her into the room*]: Why didn't you put some cold water on your chest? Do you want to catch your death of cold at your age? Did you have to hurry so?

MRS. TILFORD: Mary, what are you doing home?

[MARY *rushes to her and buries her head in* MRS. TILFORD's *dress, crying.* MRS. TILFORD *lets her cry for a moment while she pats her head, then puts an arm around the child and leads her to a sofa.*]

MRS. TILFORD: Never mind, dear; now stop crying and tell me what is the matter.

MARY [*gradually stops crying, fondling* MRS. TILFORD's *hand, playing on the older woman's affection for her*]: It's so good to see you, Grandma. You didn't come to visit me all last week.

MRS. TILFORD: I couldn't, dear. But I was coming tomorrow.

MARY: I missed you so. [*Smiling up at* MRS. TILFORD.] I was awful homesick.

MRS. TILFORD: I'm glad that's all it was. I was frightened when Agatha said you were not well.

AGATHA: Did I say that? I said she needed a good dose of rhubarb and soda. Most likely she only came home for Wednesday night fudge cake.

MRS. TILFORD: We all get homesick. But how did you

get here? Did Miss Karen drive you over?

MARY: I—I walked most of the way, and then a lady gave me a ride and—[*Looks timidly at* MRS. TILFORD.]

AGATHA: Did she have to walk through the woods in her very best coat?

MRS. TILFORD: Mary! Do you mean you left without permission?

MARY [*nervously*]: I ran away, Grandma. They didn't know—

MRS. TILFORD: That was a very bad thing to do, and they'll be worried. Agatha, phone Miss Wright and tell her Mary is here. John will drive her back before dinner.

MARY [*as* AGATHA *starts toward telephone*]: No, Grandma, don't do that. Please don't do that. Please let me stay.

MRS. TILFORD: But, darling, you can't leave school any time you please.

MARY: Oh, please, Grandma, don't send me back right away. You don't know how they'll punish me.

MRS. TILFORD: I don't think they'll be that angry. Come, you're acting like a foolish little girl.

MARY [*hysterically, as she sees* AGATHA *about to pick up the telephone*]: Grandma! Please! I can't go back! I can't! They'll kill me! They will, Grandma! They'll kill me!

[MRS. TILFORD *and* AGATHA *stare at* MARY *in amazement.*

She puts her head in MRS. TILFORD's *lap and sobs.*]

MRS. TILFORD [*motioning with a hand for* AGATHA *to leave the room*]: Never mind phoning now, Agatha.

AGATHA: If you're going to let her—

[MRS. TILFORD *repeats the gesture.* AGATHA *exits Right, with offended dignity.*]

MRS. TILFORD: Stop crying, Mary.

MARY [*raising her head from* MRS. TILFORD's *lap*]: It's so nice here, Grandma.

MRS. TILFORD: I'm glad you like being home with me, but at your age you can hardly— [*More seriously.*] What made you say such a terrible thing about Miss Wright and Miss Dobie? You know they wouldn't hurt you.

MARY: Oh, but they would. They—I— [*Breaks off, looks around as if hunting for a clue to her next word; then dramatically.*] I fainted today!

MRS. TILFORD [*alarmed*]: Fainted?

MARY: Yes, I did. My heart—I had a pain in my heart. I couldn't help having a pain in my heart, and when I fainted right in class, they called Cousin Joe and he said I didn't. He said it was maybe only that I ate my breakfast too fast and Miss Wright blamed me for it.

MRS. TILFORD [*relieved*]: I'm sure if Joseph said it wasn't serious, it wasn't.

MARY: But I did have a pain in my heart—honest.

MRS. TILFORD: Have you still got it?

MARY: I guess I haven't got it much any more, but I feel a little weak, and I was so scared of Miss Wright being so mean to me just because I was sick.

MRS. TILFORD: Scared of Karen? Nonsense. It's perfectly possible that you had a pain, but if you had really been sick your Cousin Joseph would certainly have known it. It's not nice to frighten people by pretending to be sick when you aren't.

MARY: I didn't *want* to be sick, but I'm always getting punished for everything.

MRS. TILFORD [*gently*]: You mustn't imagine things like that, child, or you'll grow up to be a very unhappy woman. I'm not going to scold you any more for coming home this time, though I suppose I should. Run along upstairs and wash your face and change your dress, and after dinner John will drive you back. Run along.

MARY [*happily*]: I can stay for dinner?

MRS. TILFORD: Yes.

MARY: Maybe I could stay till the first of the week. Saturday's your birthday and I could be here with you.

MRS. TILFORD: We don't celebrate my birthday, dear. You'll have to go back to school after dinner.

MARY: But— [*She hesitates, then goes up to* MRS. TILFORD *and puts her arms around the older woman's neck. Softly.*] How much do you love me?

MRS. TILFORD [*smiling*]: As much as all the words in

all the books in all the world.

MARY: Remember when I was little and you used to tell me that right before I went to sleep? And it was a rule nobody could say another single word after you finished? You used to say: "Wor-rr-ld," and then I had to shut my eyes tight.

MRS. TILFORD: And sometimes you were naughty and didn't shut them.

MARY: I miss you an awful lot, Grandma.

MRS. TILFORD: And I miss you, but I'm afraid my Latin is too rusty—you'll learn it better in school.

MARY: But couldn't I stay out the rest of this term? After the summer maybe I won't mind it so much. I'll study hard, honest, and——

MRS. TILFORD: You're an earnest little coaxer, but it's out of the question. Back you go tonight. [*Gives* MARY *a playful slap.*] Let's not have any more talk about it now, and let's have no more running away from school ever.

MARY [*slowly*]: Then I really have to go back there tonight?

MRS. TILFORD: Of course.

MARY: You don't love me. You don't care whether they kill me or not.

MRS. TILFORD: Mary.

MARY: You don't! You don't! You don't care what happens to me.

MRS. TILFORD [*sternly*]: But I *do* care that you're

talking this way.

MARY [*meekly*]: I'm sorry I said that, Grandma. I didn't mean to hurt your feelings. [*Puts her arms around* MRS. TILFORD'S *neck.*] Forgive me?

MRS. TILFORD: What made you talk like that?

MARY [*in a whisper*]: I'm scared, Grandma, I'm scared. They'll do dreadful things to me.

MRS. TILFORD: Dreadful? Nonsense. They'll punish you for running away. You deserve to be punished.

MARY: It's not that. It's not anything I do. It never is. They—they just punish me anyhow, just like they got something against me. I'm afraid of them, Grandma.

MRS. TILFORD: That's ridiculous. What have they ever done to you that is so terrible?

MARY: A lot of things—all the time. Miss Wright says I can't go to the boat-races and— [*Realizing the inadequacy of this reply, she breaks off, hesitates, hunting for a more telling reply, and finally stammers.*] It's—it's after what happened today.

MRS. TILFORD: You mean something else besides your naughtiness in pretending to faint and then running away?

MARY: I *did* faint. I didn't pretend. They just said that to make me feel bad. Anyway, it wasn't anything that I did.

MRS. TILFORD: What was it, then?

MARY: I can't tell you.

MRS. TILFORD: Why?

MARY [*sulkily*]: Because you're just going to take their part.

MRS. TILFORD [*a little annoyed*]: Very well. Now run upstairs and get ready for dinner.

MARY: It was—it was all about Miss Dobie and Mrs. Mortar. They were talking awful things, and Peggy and Evelyn heard them and Miss Dobie found out, and then they made us move our rooms.

MRS. TILFORD: What has that to do with you? I don't understand a word you're saying.

MARY: They made us move our rooms. They said we couldn't be together any more. They're afraid to have us near them, that's what it is, and they're taking it out on me. They're scared of you.

MRS. TILFORD: For a little girl you're imagining a lot of big things. Why should they be scared of me? Am I such an unpleasant old lady?

MARY: They're afraid you'll find out.

MRS. TILFORD: Find out what?

MARY [*vaguely*]: Things.

MRS. TILFORD: Run along, Mary. I hope you'll get more coherent as you get older.

MARY [*slowly starting for door*]: All right. But there're a lot of things. They have secrets or something, and they're afraid I'll find out and tell you.

MRS. TILFORD: There's not necessarily anything wrong with people having secrets.

MARY [*coming back in the room again*]: But they've got funny ones. Peggy and Evelyn heard Mrs. Mortar telling Miss Dobie that she was jealous of Miss Wright marrying Cousin Joe.

MRS. TILFORD: You shouldn't repeat things like that.

MARY: But that's what she said, Grandma. She said it was unnatural for a girl to feel that way.

MRS. TILFORD: What?

MARY: I'm just telling you what she said. She said there was something funny about it, and that Miss Dobie had always been like that, even when she was a little girl, and that it was unnatural—

MRS. TILFORD: Stop using that silly word, Mary.

MARY [*vaguely realizing that she is on the right track, hurries on*]: But that was the word *she* kept using, Grandma, and then they got mad and told Mrs. Mortar she'd have to get out.

MRS. TILFORD: That was probably not the reason at all.

MARY [*nodding vigorously*]: I bet it was, because honestly, Miss Dobie does get cranky and mean every time Cousin Joe comes, and today I heard her say to him: "God damn you," and then she said she was just a jealous fool and—

MRS. TILFORD: You have picked up some very fine words, haven't you, Mary?

MARY: That's just what she said, Grandma, and one time Miss Dobie was crying in Miss Wright's room, and Miss Wright was trying to stop her, and she said that

all right, maybe she wouldn't get married right away
if—

MRS. TILFORD: How do you know all this?

MARY: We couldn't help hearing because they—I mean
Miss Dobie—was talking awful loud, and their room
is right next to ours.

MRS. TILFORD: Whose room?

MARY: Miss Wright's room, I mean, and you can just
ask Peggy and Evelyn whether we didn't hear. Almost always Miss Dobie comes in after we go to bed
and stays a long time. I guess that's why they want
to get rid of us—of me—because we hear things.
That's why they're making us move our room, and
they punish me all the time for—

MRS. TILFORD: For eavesdropping, I should think. [*She
has said this mechanically. With nothing definite in
her mind, she is making an effort to conceal the fact
that* MARY's *description of the life at school has
shocked her.*] Well, now I think we've had enough
gossip, don't you? Dinner's almost ready, and I can't
eat with a girl who has such a dirty face.

MARY [*softly*]: I've heard other things, too.

MRS. TILFORD [*abstractedly*]: What? What did you say?

MARY: I've heard other things. Plenty of other things,
Grandma.

MRS. TILFORD: What things?

MARY: Bad things.

MRS. TILFORD: Well, what were they?

MARY: I can't tell you.

MRS. TILFORD: Mary, you're annoying me very much. If you have anything to say, then say it and stop acting silly.

MARY: I mean I can't say it out loud.

MRS. TILFORD: There couldn't possibly be anything so terrible that you couldn't say it out loud. Now either tell the truth or be still.

MARY: Well, a lot of things I don't understand. But it's awful, and sometimes they fight and then they make up, and Miss Dobie cries and Miss Wright gets mad, and then they make up again, and there are funny noises and we get scared.

MRS. TILFORD: Noises? I suppose you girls have a happy time imagining a murder.

MARY: And we've seen things, too. Funny things. [*Sees the impatience of her grandmother.*] I'd tell you, but I got to whisper it.

MRS. TILFORD: Why must you whisper it?

MARY: I don't know. I just got to. [*Climbs on the sofa next to* MRS. TILFORD *and begins whispering. At first the whisper is slow and hesitant, but it gradually works itself up to fast, excited talking. In the middle of it* MRS. TILFORD *stops her.*]

MRS. TILFORD [*trembling*]: Do you know what you're saying? [*Without answering,* MARY *goes back to the whispering until the older woman takes her by the shoulders and turns her around to stare in her face.*]

Mary! *Are you telling me the truth?*

MARY: Honest, honest. You just ask Peggy and Evelyn and— [*After a moment* MRS. TILFORD *gets up and begins to pace about the room. She is no longer listening to* MARY, *who keeps up a running fire of conversation.*] They know too. And maybe there're other kids who know, but we've always been frightened and so we didn't ask, and one night I was going to go and find out, but I got scared and we went to bed early so we wouldn't hear, but sometimes I couldn't help it, but we never talked about it much, because we thought they'd find out and— Oh, Grandma, don't make me go back to that awful place.

MRS. TILFORD [*abstractedly*]: What? [*Starts to move about again.*]

MARY: Don't make me go back to that place. I just couldn't stand it any more. Really, Grandma, I'm so unhappy there, and if only I could stay out the rest of the term, why, then—

MRS. TILFORD [*makes irritated gesture*]: Be still a minute. [*After a moment.*] No, you won't have to go back.

MARY [*surprised*]: Honest?

MRS. TILFORD: Honest.

MARY [*hugging* MRS. TILFORD]: You're the nicest, loveliest grandma in all the world. You—you're not mad at me?

MRS. TILFORD: I'm not mad at you. Now go upstairs and

get ready for dinner. [MARY *kisses her and runs happily out Left.* MRS. TILFORD *stands staring after her for a long moment; then, very slowly, she puts on her eyeglasses and crosses to the phone. She dials a number.*] Is Miss Wright—is Miss Wright in? [*Waits a second, hurriedly puts down the receiver.*] Never mind, never mind. [*Dials another number.*] Dr. Cardin, please. Mrs. Tilford. [*She remains absolutely motionless while she waits. When she does speak, her voice is low and tense.*] Joseph? Joseph? Can you come to see me right away? Yes, I'm perfectly well. No, but it's important, Joseph, very important. I must see you right away. I—I can't tell you over the phone. Can't you come sooner? It's not about Mary's fainting—I said it's not about Mary, Joseph; in one way it's about Mary— [*Suddenly quiet.*] But will the hospital take so long? Very well, Joseph, make it as soon as you can. [*Hangs up the receiver, sits for a moment undecided. Then, taking a breath, she dials another number.*] Mrs. Munn, please. This is Mrs. Tilford. Miriam? This is Amelia Tilford. I have something to tell you—something very shocking, I'm afraid—something about the school and Evelyn and Mary—

CURTAIN

SCENE: *The same as Scene I. The curtain has been lowered to mark the passing of a few hours.*

AT RISE: MARY *is lying on the floor playing with a puzzle.* AGATHA *appears lugging blankets and pillows across the room. Almost at the door, she stops and gives* MARY *an annoyed look.*

AGATHA: And see to it that she doesn't get my good quilt all dirty, and let her wear your green pyjamas.

MARY: Who?

AGATHA: Who? Don't you ever keep your ears open? Rosalie Wells is coming over to spend the night with you.

MARY: You mean she's going to sleep *here?*

AGATHA: You heard me.

MARY: What for?

AGATHA: Do I know all the crazy things that are happening around here? Your grandmother phoned Mrs. Wells all the way to New York, three dollars and eighty-five cents and families starving, and Mrs. Wells wanted to know if Rosalie could stay here until tomorrow.

MARY [*relieved*]: Oh. Couldn't Evelyn Munn come instead?

AGATHA: Sure. We'll have the whole town over to entertain you.

MARY: I won't let Rosalie Wells wear my new pyjamas.

AGATHA [*exits as the front door-bell rings*]: Don't tell me what you won't do. You'll act like a lady for once in your life. [*Off-stage.*] Come on in, Rosalie. Just go on in there and make yourself at home. Have you had your dinner?

ROSALIE [*off-stage*]: Good evening. Yes'm.

AGATHA [*off-stage*]: Hang up your pretty coat. Have you had your bath?

ROSALIE [*off-stage*]: Yes, ma'am. This morning.

AGATHA [*off-stage*]: Well, you better have another one. [*She is climbing the stairs as* ROSALIE *comes into the room.* MARY, *lying in front of the couch, is hidden from her. Gingerly* ROSALIE *sits down on a chair.*]

MARY [*softly*]: Whooooo. [ROSALIE *jumps.*] Whooooooo. [ROSALIE, *frightened, starts hurriedly for the door.* MARY *sits up, laughs.*] You're a goose.

ROSALIE [*belligerently*]: Oh, so it's you. Well, who likes to hear funny noises at night? You could have been a werewolf.

MARY: A werewolf wouldn't want you.

ROSALIE: You know everything, don't you? [MARY *laughs.* ROSALIE *comes over, stands staring at puzzle.*] Isn't it funny about school?

MARY: What's funny about it?

ROSALIE: Don't act like you can come home every night.

MARY: Maybe I can from now on. [*Rolls over on her back luxuriously.*] Maybe I'm never going back.

ROSALIE: Am I going back? I don't want to stay home.

MARY: What'll you give to know?

ROSALIE: Nothing. I'll ask Mamma.

MARY: Will you give me a free T. L. if I tell you?

ROSALIE [*thinks for a moment*]: All right. Lois Fisher told Helen that you were very smart.

MARY: That's an old one. I won't take it.

ROSALIE: You got to take it.

MARY: Nope.

ROSALIE [*laughs*]: You don't know, anyway.

MARY: I know what I heard, and I know Grandma phoned your mother in New York to come and get you right away. You're just going to spend the night here. I wish Evelyn could come instead of you.

ROSALIE: But what's happened? Peggy and Helen and Evelyn and Lois went home tonight, too. Do you think somebody's got scarlet fever or something?

MARY: No.

ROSALIE: Do *you* know what it is? How'd you find out? [*No answer.*] You're always pretending you know everything. You're just faking. [*Flounces away.*] Never mind, don't bother telling me. I think curiosity is very unladylike, anyhow. I have no concern with your silly secrets.

MARY: Suppose I told you that I just may have said that you were in on it?

ROSALIE: In on what?

MARY: The secret. Suppose I told you that I *may have* said that you told me about it?

ROSALIE: Why, Mary Tilford! You can't do a thing like that. I didn't tell you about anything. [MARY *laughs.*] Did you tell your grandmother such a thing?

MARY: Maybe.

ROSALIE: Did you?

MARY: Maybe.

ROSALIE: Well, I'm going right up to your grandmother and tell her I didn't tell you anything—whatever it is. You're just trying to get me into trouble and I'm not going to let you. [*Starts for door.*]

MARY: Wait a minute, I'll come with you.

ROSALIE: What for?

MARY: I want to tell her about Helen Burton's bracelet.

ROSALIE [*sits down suddenly*]: What about it?

MARY: Just that you stole it.

ROSALIE: Shut up. I didn't do any such thing.

MARY: Yes, you did.

ROSALIE [*tearfully*]: You made it up. You're always making things up.

MARY: You can't call me a fibber, Rosalie Wells. That's a kind of a dare and I won't take a dare. I guess I'll go tell Grandma, anyway. Then she can call the police and they'll come for you and you'll spend the rest of your life in one of those solitary prisons and you'll get older and older, and when you're very old and can't see anymore, they'll let you out maybe with a big sign on your back saying you're a thief, and your mother and father will be dead and you won't have any place to go and you'll beg on the streets—

ROSALIE: I didn't steal anything. I borrowed the bracelet and I was going to put it back as soon as I'd worn it to the movies. I never meant to keep it.

MARY: Nobody'll believe that, least of all the police. You're just a common, ordinary thief. Stop that bawling. You'll have the whole house down here in a minute.

ROSALIE: You won't tell? Say you won't tell.

MARY: Am I a fibber?

ROSALIE: No.

MARY: Then say: "I apologize on my hands and knees."

ROSALIE: I apologize on my hands and knees. Let's play with the puzzle.

MARY: Wait a minute. Say: "From now on, I, Rosalie Wells, am the vassal of Mary Tilford and will do and say whatever she tells me under the solemn oath of a knight."

ROSALIE: I won't say that. That's the worse oath there is. [MARY *starts for the door.*] Mary! Please don't—

MARY: Will you swear it?

ROSALIE [*sniffling*]: But then you could tell me to do anything.

MARY: And you'd have to do it. Say it quick or I'll—

ROSALIE [*hurriedly*]: From now on, I, Rosalie Wells, am the vassal of Mary Tilford and will do and say whatever she tells me under the solemn oath of a knight. [*She gasps, and sits up straight as* MRS. TILFORD *enters.*]

MARY: Don't forget that.

MRS. TILFORD: Good evening, Rosalie, you're looking very well.

ROSALIE: Good evening, Mrs. Tilford.

MARY: She's getting fatter every day.

MRS. TILFORD [*abstractedly*]: Then it's very becoming. [*Door-bell rings.*] That must be Joseph. Mary, take Rosalie into the library. There's some fruit and milk on the table. Be sure you're both fast asleep by half past ten. [*Leans down, kisses them both.* ROSALIE *starts to exit Right, sees* MARY, *stops and hesitates.*]

MARY: Go on, Rosalie. [*Waits until* ROSALIE *reluctantly exits.*] Grandma.

MRS. TILFORD: Yes?

MARY: Grandma, Cousin Joe'll say I've got to go back. He'll say I really wasn't—

[CARDIN *enters and she runs from the room.*]

CARDIN: Hello, Amelia. [*Looks curiously at the fleeing* MARY.] Mary home, eh?

MRS. TILFORD [*watching* MARY *as she leaves*]: Hello, Joseph. Sit down. [*He sits down, looks at her curiously, waits for her to speak.*] Whisky?

CARDIN: Please. How are you feeling? Headaches again?

MRS. TILFORD [*puts drink on table*]: No.

CARDIN: Those are good powders. Bicarbonate of soda and water. Never hurt anybody yet.

MRS. TILFORD: Yes. How have you been, Joseph?

CARDIN: My good health is monotonous.

MRS. TILFORD [*vaguely, sparring for time*]: I haven't seen you the last few weeks. Agatha misses you for Sunday dinners.

CARDIN: I've been busy. We're getting the results from the mating-season right about now.

MRS. TILFORD: Did I take you away from a patient?

CARDIN: No. I was at the hospital.

MRS. TILFORD: How's it getting on?

CARDIN: Just the same. No money, badly equipped, a lousy laboratory, everybody growling at everybody else— Amelia, you didn't bring me here to talk about the hospital. We're talking like people waiting for the muffins to be passed around. What's the matter with you?

MRS. TILFORD: I—I have something to tell you.

CARDIN: Well, out with it.

MRS. TILFORD: It's a very hard thing to say, Joseph.

CARDIN: Hard for you to say to *me*? [*No answer.*] Don't be worried about Mary. I guessed that she ran home to tell you about her faint. It was caused by nothing but bad temper and was very clumsily managed, at that. Amelia, she's a terribly spoilt—

MRS. TILFORD: I heard about the faint. That's not what is worrying me.

CARDIN [*gently*]: Are you in some trouble?

MRS. TILFORD: We all are in trouble. Bad trouble.

CARDIN: We? Me, you mean? Nothing's the matter with me.

MRS. TILFORD: When did you last see Karen?

CARDIN: Today. This afternoon.

MRS. TILFORD: Oh. Not since seven o'clock?

CARDIN: What's happened since seven o'clock?

MRS. TILFORD: Joseph, you've been engaged to Karen for a long time. Are your plans any more definite than they were a year ago?

CARDIN: You can get ready to buy the wedding present. We'll have the wedding here, if you don't mind. The smell of clean little girls and boiled linen would worry me.

MRS. TILFORD: Why has Karen decided so suddenly to make it definite?

CARDIN: She has not suddenly decided anything. The school is pretty well on its feet, and now that Mrs. Mortar is leaving—

MRS. TILFORD: I've heard about their putting Mrs. Mortar out.

CARDIN: Putting her out? Well, maybe. But a nice sum for a trip and a promise that a good niece will support

you the rest of your life is an enviable way of being
put out.

MRS. TILFORD [*slowly*]: Don't you find it odd, Joseph,
that they want so much to get rid of that silly, harmless woman?

CARDIN: I don't know what you're talking about, but it
isn't odd at all. Lily Mortar is not a harmless woman,
although God knows she's silly enough. She's a nasty,
tiresome, spoilt old bitch. If you're forming a Mortar
Welfare Society, you're wasting your time. [*Gets up,
puts down his glass.*] It's not like you to waste your
time. Now, what's it that's really on your mind?

MRS. TILFORD: You must not marry Karen.

CARDIN [*shocked, he grins*]: You're a very impertinent
old lady. Why must I—[*imitates her*] not marry
Karen?

MRS. TILFORD: Because there's something wrong with
Karen—something horrible.

[*The door-bell is heard to ring loud and long.*]

CARDIN: I don't think I can allow you to say things like
that, Amelia.

MRS. TILFORD: I have good reason for saying it. [*Breaks
off as she hears voices off-stage.*] Who is that?

KAREN [*off-stage*]: Mrs. Tilford, Agatha. Is she in?

AGATHA [*off-stage*]: Yes'm. Come on in.

MRS. TILFORD: I won't have her here.

CARDIN [*angrily*]: What are you talking about?

MRS. TILFORD: I won't have her here.

CARDIN [*picks up his hat*]: Then you don't want me here either. [*Turns to face* KAREN, *who, with* MARTHA, *has rushed in.*] Darling, what?—

KAREN [*stops when she sees him, puts her hand over her eyes*]: Is it a joke, Joe?

MARTHA [*with great force to* MRS. TILFORD]: We've come to find out what you are doing.

CARDIN [*kissing* KAREN]: What is it?

KAREN: It's crazy! It's crazy! What did she do it for?

CARDIN: What are you talking about? What do you mean?

MRS. TILFORD: You shouldn't have come here.

CARDIN: What is all this? What's happened?

KAREN: I tried to reach you. Hasn't she told you?

CARDIN: Nobody's told me anything. I haven't heard anything but wild talk. What is it, Karen? [*She starts to speak, then dumbly shakes her head.*] What's happened, Martha?

MARTHA [*violently*]: An insane asylum has been let loose. How do we know what's happened?

CARDIN: What was it?

KAREN: We didn't know what it was. Nobody would talk to us, nobody would tell us anything.

MARTHA: I'll tell you, I'll tell you. You see if you can make any sense out of it. At dinner-time Mrs. Munn's chauffeur said that Evelyn must be sent home right away. At half past seven Mrs. Burton arrived to tell us that she wanted Helen's things packed and that she'd wait outside because she didn't want to enter a place like ours. Five minutes later the Wells's butler came for Rosalie.

CARDIN: What was it?

MARTHA: It was madhouse. People rushing in and out, the children being pushed into cars—

KAREN [*quiet now, takes his hand*]: Mrs. Rogers finally told us.

CARDIN: What? What?

KAREN: That—that Martha and I have been—have been lovers. Mrs. Tilford told them.

CARDIN [*for a moment stands staring at her incredulously. Then he walks across the room, stares out of the window, and finally turns to* MRS. TILFORD]: Did you tell them that?

MRS. TILFORD: Yes.

CARDIN: Are you sick?

MRS. TILFORD: You know I'm not sick.

CARDIN [*snapping the words out*]: Then what did you do it for?

MRS. TILFORD [*slowly*]: Because it's true.

KAREN [*incredulously*]: You think it's true, then?

MARTHA: You fool! You damned, vicious—

KAREN: Do you realize what you're saying?

MRS. TILFORD: I realize it very well. And—

MARTHA: You realize nothing, nothing, nothing.

MRS. TILFORD: And that's why I don't think you should

have come here. [*Quietly, with a look at* MARTHA.]
I shall not call you names, and I will not allow you to
call me names. It comes to this: I can't trust myself
to talk about it with you now or ever.

KAREN: What's she talking about, Joe? What's she
mean? What is she trying to do to us? What is everybody doing to us?

MARTHA [*softly, as though to herself*]: Pushed around.
We're being pushed around by crazy people. [*Shakes
herself slightly.*] That's an awful thing. And we're
standing here— [CARDIN *puts his arm around* KAREN,
*walks with her to the window. They stand there to-
gether.*] We're standing here taking it. [*Suddenly
with violence.*] Didn't you know we'd come here?
Were we supposed to lie down and grin while you
kicked us around with these lies?

MRS. TILFORD: This can't do any of us any good, Miss
Dobie.

MARTHA [*scornfully imitating her*]: "This can't do any
of us any good." Listen, listen. Try to understand this:
you're not playing with paper dolls. We're human
beings, see? It's our lives you're fooling with. *Our*
lives. That's serious business for us. Can you understand that?

MRS. TILFORD [*for the first time she speaks angrily*]: I
can understand that, and I understand a lot more.
You've been playing with a lot of children's lives, and
that's why I stopped you. [*More calmly.*] I know

how serious this is for you, how serious it is for all
of us.

CARDIN [*bitterly*]: I don't think you do know.

MRS. TILFORD: I wanted to avoid this meeting because it
can't do any good. You came here to find out if I had
made the charge. You've found out. Let's end it
there. *I don't want you in this house.* I'm sorry this
had to be done to you, Joseph.

CARDIN: I don't like your sympathy.

MRS. TILFORD: Very well. There's nothing I mean to do,
nothing I want to do. There's nothing anybody can do.

CARDIN [*carefully*]: You have already done a terrible
thing.

MRS. TILFORD: I have done what I had to do. What they
are may possibly be their own business. It becomes a
great deal more than that when children are involved.

KAREN [*wildly*]: It's not true. Not a word of it is true;
can't you understand that?

MRS. TILFORD: There won't be any punishment for either
of you. But there mustn't be any punishment for me,
either—and that's what this meeting is. This—this
thing is your own. Go away with it. I don't understand it and I don't want any part of it.

MARTHA [*slowly*]: So you thought we would go away?

MRS. TILFORD: I think that's best for you.

MARTHA: There must be something we can do to you,
and, whatever it is, we'll find it.

MRS. TILFORD: That will be very unwise.

KAREN: You are right to be afraid.

MRS. TILFORD: I am not afraid, Karen.

CARDIN: But you *are* old—and you *are* irresponsible.

MRS. TILFORD [*hurt*]: You know that's not true.

KAREN [*goes to her*]: I don't want to have anything to do with your mess, do you hear me? It makes me feel dirty and sick to be forced to say this, but here it is: there isn't a single word of truth in anything you've said. We're standing here defending ourselves—and against what? Against a lie. A great, awful lie.

MRS. TILFORD: I'm sorry that I can't believe that.

KAREN: Damn you!

CARDIN: But you can believe this: they've worked eight long years to save enough money to buy that farm, to start that school. They did without everything that young people ought to have. You wouldn't know about that. That school meant things to them: self-respect, and bread and butter, and honest work. Do you know what it is to try so hard for anything? Well, now it's gone. [*Suddenly hits the side of the table with his hand.*] What the hell did you do it for?

MRS. TILFORD [*softly*]: It had to be done.

CARDIN: Righteousness is a great thing.

MRS. TILFORD [*gently*]: I know how you must feel.

CARDIN: You don't know anything about how I feel. And you don't know how they feel, either.

MRS. TILFORD: I've loved you as much as I loved my own

boys. I wouldn't have spared them; I couldn't spare you.

CARDIN [*fiercely*]: I believe you.

MARTHA: What is there to do to you? What can we do to you? There must be something—something that makes you feel the way we do tonight. You don't want any part of this, you said. But you'll get a part. More than you bargained for. [*Suddenly.*] Listen: are you willing to stand by everything you've said tonight?

MRS. TILFORD: Yes.

MARTHA: All right. That's fine. But don't get the idea we'll let you whisper this lie: you made it and you'll come out with it. Shriek it to your town of Lancet. We'll *make* you shriek it—and we'll make you do it in a court room. [*Quietly.*] Tomorrow, Mrs. Tilford, you will have a libel suit on your hands.

MRS. TILFORD: That will be very unwise.

KAREN: Very unwise—for you.

MRS. TILFORD: It is you I am thinking of. I am frightened for you. It was wrong of you to brazen it out here tonight; it would be criminally foolish of you to brazen it out in public. That can bring you nothing but pain. I am an old woman, Miss Dobie, and I have seen too many people, out of pride, act on that pride. In the end they punish themselves.

MARTHA: And you feel that you are too old to be punished? That we should spare you?

MRS. TILFORD: You know that is not what I meant.

CARDIN [*turns from the window*]: So you took a child's word for it?

MARTHA [*looks at him, shakes her head*]: I knew it, too.

KAREN: That is really where you got it? I can't believe —it couldn't be. Why, she's a child.

MARTHA: She's not a child any longer.

KAREN: Oh, my God, it all fits so well now. That girl has hated us for a long time. We never knew why, we never could find out. There didn't seem to be any reason—

MARTHA: There wasn't any reason. She hates everybody and everything.

KAREN: Your Mary's a strange girl, a bad girl. There's something very awful the matter with her.

MRS. TILFORD: I was waiting for you to say that, Miss Wright.

KAREN: I'm telling you the truth. We should have told it to you long ago. [*Stops, sighs.*] It's no use.

MARTHA: Where is she? Bring her out here and let us hear what she has to say.

MRS. TILFORD: You cannot see her.

CARDIN: Where is she?

MRS. TILFORD: I won't have that, Joseph.

CARDIN: I'm going to talk to her.

MRS. TILFORD: *I won't have her go through with that again.* [*To* KAREN *and* MARTHA.] You came here demanding explanations. It was I who should have asked them from you. You attack me, you attack Mary. I've told you I didn't mean you any harm. I still don't. You claim that it isn't true; it may be natural that you should say that, but I *know* that it is true. No matter what you say, you know very well that I wouldn't have acted until I was absolutely sure. All I wanted was to get those children away. That has been done. There won't be any talk about it or about you—I'll see to that. You have been in my house long enough. Get out.

KAREN [*gets up*]: The wicked very young, and the wicked very old. Let's go home.

CARDIN: Sit down. [*To* MRS. TILFORD.] When two people come here with their lives spread on the table for you to cut to pieces, then the only honest thing to do is to give them a chance to come out whole. Are you honest?

MRS. TILFORD: I've always thought so.

CARDIN: Then where is Mary? [*After a moment she moves her head to door Right. Quickly* CARDIN *goes to the door and opens it.*] Mary! Come here.

[*After a moment* MARY *appears, stands nervously near door. Her manner is shy and afraid.*]

MRS. TILFORD [*gently*]: Sit down, dear, and don't be afraid.

MARTHA [*her lips barely moving*]: *Make* her tell the truth.

CARDIN [*walking about in front of* MARY]: Look: every-

body lies all the time. Sometimes they have to, sometimes they don't. I've lied myself for a lot of different
reasons, but there was never a time when, if I'd been
given a second chance, I wouldn't have taken back the
lie and told the truth. You're lucky if you ever get
that chance. I'm telling you this because I'm about to
ask you a question. Before you answer the question, I
want to tell you that if you've l——, if you made a mis-
take, you must take this chance and say so. You won't
be punished for it. Do you get all that?

MARY [*timidly*]: Yes, Cousin Joe.

CARDIN [*grimly*]: All right, let's get started. Were you
telling your grandmother the truth this afternoon?
The exact truth about Miss Wright and Miss Dobie?

MARY [*without hesitation*]: Oh, yes.

[KAREN *sighs deeply,* MARTHA, *her fists closed tight,
turns her back to the child.* CARDIN *smiles as he looks
at* MARY.]

CARDIN: All right, Mary, that was your chance; you
passed it up. [*Pulls up a chair, sits down in front of
her.*] Now let's find out things.

MRS. TILFORD: She's told you. Aren't you through?

CARDIN: Not by a long shot. You've started something,
and I'm going to finish it for you. Will you answer
some more questions, Mary?

MARY: Yes, Cousin Joe.

MARTHA: Stop that sick, sweet tone.

[MRS. TILFORD *half rises;* CARDIN *motions her back.*]

CARDIN: Why don't you like Miss Dobie and Miss Wright?

MARY: Oh, I do like them. They just don't like me. They never have liked me.

CARDIN: How do you know?

MARY: They're always picking on me. They're always punishing me for everything that happens. No matter what happens, it's always me.

CARDIN: Why do you think they do that?

MARY: Because—because they're—because they— [*Stops, turns.*] Grandma, I—

CARDIN: All right, we'll skip that one. Did you get punished today?

MARY: Yes, and it was just because Peggy and Evelyn heard them and so they took it out on me.

KAREN: That's a lie.

CARDIN: Sssh. Heard what, Mary?

MARY: Mrs. Mortar told Miss Dobie that there was something funny about her. She said that she had a funny feeling about Miss Wright, and Mrs. Mortar said that was unnatural. That was why we got punished, just because—

KAREN: That was not the reason they got punished.

MRS. TILFORD [*to* MARTHA]: Miss Dobie?

MARTHA: My aunt is a stupid woman. What she said was unpleasant; it was said to annoy me. It meant nothing more than that.

MARY: And, Cousin Joe, she said that every time you

came to the school Miss Dobie got jealous, and that she didn't want you to get married.

MARTHA [*to* CARDIN]: She said that, too. For God's sake, can't you see what's happening? This—this child is taking little things, little family things, and making them have meanings that— [*Stops, suddenly regards* MARY *with a combination of disgust and interest.*] Where did you learn so much in so little time?

CARDIN: What do you think Mrs. Mortar meant by all that, Mary?

MRS. TILFORD: Stop it, Joseph!

MARY: I don't know, but it was always kind of funny and she always said things like that and all the girls would talk about it when Miss Dobie went and visited Miss Wright late at night—

KAREN [*angrily*]: And we go to the movies at night and sometimes we read at night and sometimes we drink tea at night. Those are guilty things, too, Mrs. Tilford.

MARY: And there are always funny sounds and we'd stay awake and listen because we couldn't help hearing and I'd get frightened because the sounds were like—

MARTHA: Be still!

KAREN [*with violence*]: No, no. You don't want her still now. What else did you hear?

MARY: Grandma, I—

MRS. TILFORD [*bitterly to* CARDIN]: You are trying to make her name it, aren't you?

CARDIN [*ignoring her, speaks to* MARY]: Go on.

MARY: I don't know; there were just sounds.

CARDIN: But what did you think they were? Why did they frighten you?

MARY [*weakly*]: I don't know.

CARDIN [*smiles at* MRS. TILFORD]: She doesn't know.

MARY [*hastily*]: I saw things, too. One night there was so much noise I thought somebody was sick or something and I looked through the keyhole and they were kissing and saying things and then I got scared because it was different sort of and I—

MARTHA [*her face distorted, turns to* MRS. TILFORD]: That child—that child is sick.

KAREN: Ask her again how she could see us.

CARDIN: How could you see Miss Dobie and Miss Wright?

MARY: I—I—

MRS. TILFORD: Tell him what you whispered to me.

MARY: It was at night and I was leaning down by the keyhole.

KAREN: *There's no keyhole on my door.*

MRS. TILFORD: What?

KAREN: There—is—no—keyhole—on—my—door.

MARY [*quickly*]: It wasn't her room, Grandma, it was the other room, I guess. It was *Miss Dobie's* room. I saw them through the keyhole in Miss Dobie's room.

CARDIN: How did you know anybody was in Miss Dobie's room?

MARY: I told you, I told you. Because we heard them. Everybody heard them—

MARTHA: I share a room with my aunt. It is on the first floor at the other end of the house. It is impossible to hear anything from there. [*To* CARDIN.] Tell her to come and see for herself.

MRS. TILFORD [*her voice shaken*]: What is this, Mary? Why did you say you saw through a keyhole? *Can* you hear from your room?—

MARY [*starts to cry*]: Everybody is yelling at me. I don't know what I'm saying with everybody mixing me all up. I did see it! I did see it!

MRS. TILFORD: *What* did you see? *Where* did you see it? I want the truth, now. The truth, whatever it is.

CARDIN [*gets up, moves his chair back*]: We can go home. We are finished here. [*Looks around.*] It's not a pleasant place to be.

MRS. TILFORD [*angrily*]: Stop that crying, Mary. Stand up.

[MARY *gets up, head down, still crying hysterically.* MRS. TILFORD *goes and stands directly in front of her.*]

MRS. TILFORD: *I want the truth.*

MARY: All—all right.

MRS. TILFORD: What is the truth?

MARY: It was Rosalie who saw them. I just said it was me so I wouldn't have to tattle on Rosalie.

CARDIN [*wearily*]: Oh, my God!

MARY: It *was* Rosalie, Grandma, she told us all about it.

She said she had read about it in a book and she knew—

CARDIN [*picks up his hat*]: We'll go now. Good night, Amelia, and good-by.

MARY [*desperately*]: You ask Rosalie. You just ask Rosalie. She'll tell you. We used to talk about it all the time. That's the truth, that's the honest truth. She said it was when the door was open once and she ·told us all about it. I was just trying to save Rosalie, and everybody jumps on me.

MRS. TILFORD [*to* CARDIN]: Please wait a minute. [*Goes to library door.*] Rosalie!

CARDIN: You're giving yourself an awful beating, Amelia, and you deserve whatever you get.

MRS. TILFORD [*stands waiting for* ROSALIE, *passes her hand over her face*]: I don't know. I don't know, any more. Maybe it's what I do deserve. [*As* ROSALIE, *frightened, appears at the door, making bows to every-body, she takes the child gently by the hand, brings her down Center, talking nervously.*] I'm sorry to keep you up so late, Rosalie. You must be tired. [*Speaks rapidly.*] Mary says there's been a lot of talk in the school lately about Miss Wright and Miss Dobie. Is that true?

ROSALIE: I—I don't know what you mean.

MRS. TILFORD: That things have been said among you girls.

ROSALIE [*wide-eyed, frightened*]: What things? I never —I—I—

KAREN [*gently*]: Don't be frightened.

MRS. TILFORD: What was the talk about, Rosalie?

ROSALIE [*utterly bewildered*]: I don't know what she means, Miss Wright.

KAREN: Rosalie, Mary has told her grandmother that certain things at school have been—er—puzzling you girls. You, particularly.

ROSALIE: History puzzles me. I guess I'm not very good at history, and Helen helps me sometimes, if that—

KAREN: No, that's not what she meant. She says that you told her that you saw certain—certain acts between Miss Dobie and myself. She says that once, when the door was open, you saw us kissing each other in a way that—[*Unable to bear the child's look, she turns her back.*] women don't kiss one another.

ROSALIE: Oh, Miss Wright, I didn't, didn't, I didn't. I *never* said such a thing.

MRS. TILFORD [*grimly*]: That's true, my dear?

ROSALIE: I never saw any such thing. Mary always makes things up about me and everybody else. [*Starts to weep in excitement.*] I never said any such thing ever. Why, I never even could have thought of—

MARY [*staring at her, speaks very slowly*]: Yes, you did, Rosalie. You're just trying to get out of it. I remember just when you said it. I remember it, because it was the day Helen Burton's bracelet was—

ROSALIE [*stands fascinated and fearful, looking at MARY*]: I never did. I—I—you're just—

MARY: It was the day Helen's bracelet was stolen, and nobody knew who did it, and Helen said that if her mother found out, she'd have the thief put in jail.

KAREN [*puzzled, as are the others, by the sudden change in* ROSALIE's *manner*]: There's nothing to cry about. You must help us by telling the truth. Why, what's the matter, Rosalie?

MARY: Grandma, there's something I've got to tell you that—

ROSALIE [*with a shrill cry*]: Yes. Yes. I did see it. I told Mary. What Mary said was right. I said it, I said it—

[*Throws herself on the couch, weeping hysterically;* MARTHA *stands leaning against the door;* KAREN, CARDIN, *and* MRS. TILFORD *are staring at* ROSALIE; MARY *slowly sits down as the Curtain falls.*]

ACT III

SCENE: *The same as Act One. Living-room of the
school.*

AT RISE: *The room has changed. It is not actually
dirty, but it is dull and dark and uncared for. The win-
dows are tightly shut, the curtains tightly drawn.*
KAREN *is sitting in a large chair, Right Center, feet flat
on floor.* MARTHA *is lying on the couch, her face buried
against the pillows, her back to* KAREN. *It is a minute
or two after the rise of the curtain before either speaks.*

MARTHA: It's cold in here.
KAREN: Yes.
MARTHA: What time is it?
KAREN: I don't know. What's the difference?
MARTHA: None. I was hoping it was time for my bath.
KAREN: Take it early today.
MARTHA [*laughs*]: Oh, I couldn't do that. I look for-
ward all day to that bath. It's my last touch with the
full life. It makes me feel important to know that
there's one thing ahead of me, one thing I've *got* to
do. You ought to get yourself something like that.
I tell you, at five o'clock every day you comb your
hair. How's that? It's better for you, take my word.
You wake up in the morning and you say to yourself,

85

the day's not entirely empty, life is rich and full: at five o'clock I'll comb my hair.

[*They fall back into silence. A moment later the phone rings. Neither of them pays the slightest attention to it, until the ringing becomes too insistent. Then* KAREN *rises, takes the receiver off, goes back, and sits down.*]

KAREN: It's raining.

MARTHA: Hungry?

KAREN: No. You?

MARTHA: No, but I'd like to be hungry again. Remember how much we used to eat at college?

KAREN: That was ten years ago.

MARTHA: Well, maybe we'll be hungry in another ten years. It's cheaper this way.

KAREN: What's the old thing about time being more nourishing than bread?

MARTHA: Yeah? Maybe.

KAREN: Joe's late today. What time is it?

MARTHA [*turns again to lie on her side*]: We've been sitting here for eight days asking each other the time. Haven't you heard? There isn't any time any more.

KAREN: It's been days since we've been out of this house.

MARTHA: Well, we'll have to get off these chairs sooner or later. In a couple of months they'll need dusting.

KAREN: What'll we do when we get off?

MARTHA: God knows.

KAREN [*almost in a whisper*]: It's awful.

MARTHA: Let's not talk about it. [*After a moment.*]

What about eggs for dinner?

KAREN: All right.

MARTHA: I'll make some potatoes with onions, the way you used to like them.

KAREN: It's a week ago Thursday. It never seemed real until the last day. It seems real enough now, all right.

MARTHA: Now and forever after.

KAREN [*suddenly*]: Let's go out.

MARTHA [*turns over, stares at her*]: Where to?

KAREN: We'll take a walk.

MARTHA: Where'll we walk?

KAREN: Why shouldn't we take a walk? We won't see anybody, and suppose we do, what of it? We'll jus—

MARTHA [*slowly gets up*]: Come on. We'll go through the park.

KAREN: They might see us. [*They stand looking at each other.*] Let's not go. [MARTHA *goes back, lies down again.*] We'll go tomorrow.

MARTHA [*laughs*]: Stop kidding yourself.

KAREN: But Joe says we've got to go out. He says that all the people who don't think it's true will begin to wonder if we keep hiding this way.

MARTHA: If it makes you feel better to think there *are* such people, go ahead.

KAREN: He says we ought to go into town and go shopping and act as though—

MARTHA: Shopping? That's a sound idea. There aren't three stores in Lancet that would sell us anything.

Hasn't he heard about the ladies' clubs and their meetings and their circulars and their visits and their—

KAREN [*softly*]: Don't tell him.

MARTHA [*gently*]: I won't. [*There are footsteps in the hall, and the sound of something being dragged.*] There's our friend.

[*A* GROCERY BOY *appears lugging a box. He brings it into the room, stands staring at them, giggles a little. Walks toward* KAREN, *stops, examines her. She sits tense, looking away from him. Without taking his eyes from* KAREN, *he speaks.*]

GROCERY BOY: I knocked on the kitchen door, but nobody answered.

MARTHA: You said that yesterday. All right. Thanks. Good-by.

KAREN [*unable any longer to stand the stare*]: Make him stop it.

GROCERY BOY: Here are the things. [*Giggles, moves toward* MARTHA, *stands looking at her. Suddenly* MARTHA *thrusts her hand in the air.*]

MARTHA: I've got eight fingers, see? I'm a freak.

GROCERY BOY [*giggling*]: There's a car comin' here. [*Gets no answer, starts backing out of door, still looking. Familiarly.*] Good-by. [*Exits.*]

MARTHA [*bitterly*]: You still think we should go into town?

KAREN: I don't know. I don't know about anything any

more. [*After a moment.*] Martha, Martha, Martha—

MARTHA [*gently*]: What is it, Karen?

KAREN: What are we going to do? It's all so cold and unreal and awful. It's like that dark hour of the night when, half awake, you struggle through the black mess you've been dreaming. Then, suddenly, you wake up and you see your own bed or your own nightgown and you know you're back again in a solid world. But now it's all the nightmare; there is no solid world. Oh, Martha, *why* did it happen? *What* happened? What are we doing here like this?

MARTHA: Waiting.

KAREN: For what?

MARTHA: I don't know.

KAREN: We've got to get out of this place. I can't stand it any more.

MARTHA: You'll be getting married soon. Everything will be all right then.

KAREN [*vaguely*]: Yes.

MARTHA [*looks up at the tone*]: What is it?

KAREN: Nothing.

MARTHA: There mustn't be anything wrong between you and Joe. Never.

KAREN [*without conviction*]: Nothing's wrong. [*As footsteps are heard in the hall, her face lights up.*] There's Joe now.

[MRS. MORTAR, *small suitcase in hand, stands in the doorway, her face pushed coyly forward.*]

MRS. MORTAR: And here I am. Hello, hello.

MARTHA [*she has turned over on her back and is staring at her aunt. She speaks to* KAREN]: The Duchess, isn't it? Returned at long last. [*Too jovially.*] Come on in. We're delighted to see you. Are you tired from your journey? Is there something I can get you?

MRS. MORTAR [*surprised*]: I'm very glad to see you both, and [*looks around*] I'm very glad to see the old place again. How is everything?

MARTHA: Everything's fine. We're splendid, thank you. You're just in time for tea.

MRS. MORTAR: You know, I should like some tea, if it isn't too much trouble.

MARTHA: No trouble at all. Some small sandwiches and a little brandy?

MRS. MORTAR [*puzzled finally*]: Why, Martha.

MARTHA: Where the hell have you been?

MRS. MORTAR: Around, around. I had a most interesting time. Things—

MARTHA: Why didn't you answer my telegrams?

MRS. MORTAR: Things have changed in the theater— drastically changed, I might say.

MARTHA: *Why didn't you answer my telegrams?*

MRS. MORTAR: Oh, Martha, there's your temper again.

MARTHA: Answer me and don't bother about my temper.

MRS. MORTAR [*nervously*]: I was moving around a great deal. [*Conversationally.*] You know, I think it will throw a very revealing light on the state of the new theater when I tell you that the Lyceum in Rochester now has a toilet back-stage.

MARTHA: To hell with the toilet in Rochester. Where were you?

MRS. MORTAR: Moving around, I tell you.

KAREN: What difference does it all make now?

MRS. MORTAR: Karen is quite right. Let bygones be bygones. As I was saying, there's an effete something in the theater now, and that accounts for—

MARTHA [to KAREN]: Isn't she wonderful? [To MRS. MORTAR.] Why did you refuse to come back here and testify for us?

MRS. MORTAR: Why, Martha, I didn't refuse to come back at all. That's the wrong way to look at it. I was on a tour; that's a moral obligation, you know. Now don't let's talk about unpleasant things any more. I'll go up and unpack a few things; tomorrow's plenty of time to get my trunk.

KAREN [laughs]: Things have changed here, you know.

MARTHA: She doesn't know. She expected to walk right up to a comfortable fire and sit down and she very carefully waited until the whole thing was over. [Leans forward, speaking to MRS. MORTAR.] Listen: Karen Wright and Martha Dobie brought a libel suit against a woman called Tilford because her grandchild had accused them of having what the judge called "sinful sexual knowledge of one another." [MRS. MORTAR holds up her hand in protest, and

MARTHA *laughs*.] Don't like that, do you? Well, a great part of the defense's case was based on remarks made by Lily Mortar, actress in the toilets of Rochester, against her niece, Martha. And a greater part of the defense's case rested on the telling fact that Mrs. Mortar would not appear in court to deny or explain those remarks. Mrs. Mortar had a moral obligation to the theater. As you probably read in the papers, we lost the case.

MRS. MORTAR: I didn't think of it that way, Martha. It couldn't have done any good for all of us to get mixed up in that unpleasant notoriety— [*Sees* MARTHA'S *face. Hastily*] But now that you've explained it, why, I do see it your way, and I'm sorry I didn't come back. But now that I am here, I'm going to stand shoulder to shoulder with you. I know what you've gone through, but the body and heart *do* recover, you know. I'll be here working right along with you and we'll—

MARTHA: There's an eight o'clock train. Get on it.

MRS. MORTAR: Martha.

MARTHA: You've come back to pick the bones dry. Well, there aren't even bones anymore. There's nothing here for you.

MRS. MORTAR [*sniffling a little*]: How can you talk to me like that?

MARTHA: Because I hate you. I've always hated you.

MRS. MORTAR [*gently*]: God will punish you for that.

MARTHA: He's been doing all right.

MRS. MORTAR: When you wish to apologize, I will be temporarily in my room. [*Starts to exit, almost bumps into* CARDIN, *steps back with dignity.*] How do you do?

CARDIN [*laughs*]: Look who's here. A little late, aren't you?

MRS. MORTAR: So it's you. Now, I call *that* loyal. A lot of men wouldn't still be here. They would have felt—

MARTHA: Get out of here.

KAREN [*opening door*]: I'll call you when it's time for your train.

[MRS. MORTAR *looks at her, exits.*]

CARDIN: Now, what do you think brought her back?

KAREN: God knows.

MARTHA: I know. She was broke.

CARDIN [*pats* MARTHA *on the shoulder*]: Don't let her worry you this time, Martha. We'll give her some money and get rid of her. [*Pulls* KAREN *to him.*] Been out today, darling?

KAREN: We started to go out.

CARDIN [*shakes his head*]: Feel all right?

[KAREN *leans over to kiss him. Almost imperceptibly he pulls back.*]

KAREN: Why did you do that?

MARTHA: Karen.

CARDIN: Do what?

KAREN: Draw back that way.

CARDIN [*laughs, kisses her*]: If we sit around here much

longer, we'll all be bats. I sold my place today to Foster.

KAREN: You did what?

CARDIN: We're getting married this week. Then we're going away—all three of us.

KAREN: You can't leave here. I won't have you do this for me. What about the hospital and—

CARDIN: Shut up, darling, it's all fixed. We're going to Vienna and we're going quick. Fischer wrote that I can have my old place back.

KAREN: No! No! I'm not going to let you.

CARDIN: It's already done. Fischer can't pay me much, but it'll be enough for the three of us. Plenty if we live cheap.

MARTHA: I couldn't go with you, Joe.

CARDIN: Nonsense, Martha, we're all going. We're going to have fun again.

KAREN [slowly]: You don't want to go back to Vienna.

CARDIN: No.

KAREN: Then why?

CARDIN: Look: I don't want to go to Vienna; I'd rather have stayed here. But then you don't want to go to Vienna; you'd rather have stayed here. Well, to hell with that. We *can't* stay here, and Vienna offers enough to eat and sleep and drink beer on. Now don't object any more, please, darling. All right?

KAREN: All right.

MARTHA: I can't go. It's better for all of us if I don't.

CARDIN [*puts his arm around her*]: Not now. You stay with us now. Later on, if you want it that way. All right?

MARTHA [*smiles*]: All right.

CARDIN: Swell. I'll buy you good coffee cakes and take you both to Ischl for a honeymoon.   .

MARTHA [*picking up grocery box, she starts for door*]: A big coffee cake with a lot of raisins. It would be nice to like something again. [*Exits.*]

CARDIN [*with a slightly forced heartiness*]: I'll be going back with a pretty girl who belongs to me. I'll show you off all over the place—to Dr. Engelhardt, and the nurse at the desk, and to the fat gal in the cake shop, and to Fischer. [*Laughs.*] The last time I saw him was at the railroad station. He took me back of the baggage car. [*With an imitation of an accent.*] "Joseph," he said, "you'll be a good doctor; I would trust you to cut up my Minna. But you're not a great doctor, and you never will be. Go back where you were born and take care of your sick. Leave the fancy work to the others." I came home.

KAREN: You'll be coming home again some day.

CARDIN: No. Let's not talk about it. [*After a moment.*] You'll need some clothes?

KAREN: A few. Oh, your Dr. Fischer was so right. This is where you belong.

CARDIN: I need an overcoat and a suit. You'll need a lot of things—heavy things. It's cold there now, much colder than you'd expect—

KAREN: I've done this to you. I've taken you away from everything you want.

CARDIN: But it's lovely in the mountains, and that's where we'll go for a month.

KAREN: They—*they've* done it. They've taken away every chance we had. Everything we wanted, everything we were going to be.

CARDIN: And we've got to stop talking like that. [*Takes her by the shoulders.*] We've got a chance. But it's just one chance, and if we miss it we're done for. It means that we've got to start putting the whole business behind us now. *Now,* Karen. What you've done, you've done—and that's that.

KAREN: What *I've* done?

CARDIN [*impatiently*]: What's been done to you.

KAREN: What did you mean? [*When there is no answer.*] What did you mean when you said: "What you've done"?

CARDIN [*shouting*]: Nothing. Nothing. [*Then very quietly.*] Karen, there are a lot of people in this world who've had bad trouble in their lives. We're three of those people. We could sit around the rest of our lives and exist on that trouble, until in the end we had nothing else and we'd want nothing else. That's something I'm not coming to and I'm not going to let you come to.

KAREN: I know. I'm sorry. [*After a moment.*] Joe, can

we have a baby right away?

CARDIN [*vaguely*]: Yes, I guess so. Although we won't have much money now.

KAREN: You used to want one right away. You always said that was the way you wanted it. There's some reason for your changing.

CARDIN: My God, we *can't* go on like this. Everything I say to you is made to mean something else. We don't talk like people any more. Oh, let's get out of here as fast as we can.

KAREN [*as though she is finishing the sentence for him*]: And every word will have a new meaning. You think we'll be able to run away from that? Woman, child, love, lawyer—no words that we can use in safety any more. [*Laughs bitterly.*] Sick, high-tragic people. That's what we'll be.

CARDIN [*gently*]: No, we won't, darling. Love is casual —that's the way it should be. We must find that out all over again. We must learn again to live and love like other people.

KAREN: It won't work.

CARDIN: What?

KAREN: The two of us together.

CARDIN [*sharply*]: Stop talking like that.

KAREN: It's true. [*Suddenly.*] I want you to say it now.

CARDIN: I don't know what you're talking about.

KAREN: Yes, you do. We've both known for a long time. I knew surely the day we lost the case. I was watching your face in court. It was ashamed—and sad at being ashamed. Say it now, Joe. Ask it now.

CARDIN: I have nothing to ask. Nothing— [*Quickly.*] All right. Is it—was it ever—

KAREN [*puts her hand over his mouth*]: No. Martha and I have never touched each other. [*Pulls his head down on her shoulder.*] That's all right, darling. I'm glad you asked. I'm not mad a bit, really.

CARDIN: I'm sorry, Karen, I'm sorry. I didn't mean to hurt you, I—

KAREN: I'll say it for you. You wanted to wait until it was all over, you really never wanted to ask at all. You didn't know for sure; you thought there might be just a little truth in it all. [*With great feeling.*] You've been good to me and loyal. You're a fine man. [*Afraid of tears, she pats him, walks away.*] Now go and sit down, Joe. I have a lot of things to say. They're all mixed up and I must get them clear.

CARDIN: Don't let's talk any more. Let's forget and go ahead.

KAREN [*puzzled*]: Go ahead?

CARDIN: Yes, Karen.

KAREN: You believe me, then?

CARDIN: Of course I believe you. I only had to hear you say it.

KAREN: No, no, no. That isn't the way things work. Maybe you believe me. I'd never know whether you did or not. You'd never know whether you did, either.

We couldn't do it that way. Can't you see what would happen? We'd be hounded by it all our lives. I'd be frightened, always, and in the end my own fright would make me—would make me hate you. [*Sees slight movement he makes.*] Yes, it would; I know it would. I'd hate you for what I thought I'd done to you. And I'd hate myself, too. It would grow and grow until we'd be ruined by it. [*Sees him about to speak.*] Ah, Joe, you've seen all that yourself. You knew it first.

CARDIN [*softly*]: I didn't mean it that way; I don't now.

KAREN [*smiles*]: You're still trying to spare me, still trying to tell yourself that we might be all right again. But we won't be all right. Not ever, ever, ever. I don't know all the reasons why. Look, I'm standing here. I haven't changed. [*Holds out her hands.*] My hands look just the same, my face is the same, even my dress is old. We're in a room we've been in so many times before; you're sitting where you always sit; it's nearly time for dinner. I'm like everybody else. I can have all the things that everybody has. I can have you and a baby, and I can go to market, and we can go to the movies, and people will talk to me and— [*Suddenly notices the pain in his face.*] Oh, I'm sorry. I mustn't talk like that. That couldn't be true any more.

CARDIN: It could be, Karen. We'll make it be like that.

KAREN: No. That's only what we'd like to have had. It's

what we can't have now. Go home, darling.

CARDIN [*with force*]: Don't talk like that. No matter what it is, we can't leave each other. I can't leave you—

KAREN: Joe, Joe. Let's do it now and quick; it will be too hard later on.

CARDIN: No, no, no. We love each other. [*His voice breaks.*] I'd give anything not to have asked that question, Karen.

KAREN: It had to be asked sooner or later—and answered. You're a good man—the best I'll ever know —and you've been better to me than— But it's no good now, for either of us; you can see that.

CARDIN: It can be. You say I helped you. Help me now; help me to be strong and good enough to— [*Goes towards her with his arms out.*] Karen!

KAREN [*drawing back*]: No, Joe! [*Then, as he stops*] Will you do something for me?

CARDIN: Anything but leave you.

KAREN: Will you—will you go away for two days—a day—and think this all over by yourself—away from me and love and pity? Will you? And then decide.

CARDIN [*after a long pause*]: Yes, if you want, but it won't make any difference. We will—

KAREN: Don't say anything. Please go now. [*She sits down, smiles, closes her eyes. For a moment he stands looking at her, then slowly puts on his hat.*] And all my heart goes with you.

CARDIN [*at door, leaving*]: I'll be coming back. [*Exits, slowly, reluctantly, closing door.*]

KAREN [*a moment after he has gone*]: No, you won't. Never, darling. [*Stays as she is until* MARTHA *enters Right.*]

MARTHA [*goes to lamp, lights it*]: It gets dark so early now. [*Sits down, stretches, laughs.*] Cooking always makes me feel better. Well, I guess we'll have to give the Duchess some dinner. When the hawks descend, you've got to feed 'em. Where's Joe? [*No answer.*] Where's Joe?

KAREN: Gone.

MARTHA: A patient? Will he be back in time for dinner?

KAREN: No.

MARTHA [*watching her*]: We'll save dinner for him, then. Karen! What's the matter?

KAREN [*in a dull tone*]: He won't be back any more.

MARTHA [*speaking slowly and carefully*]: You mean he won't be back any more tonight.

KAREN: He won't be back at all.

MARTHA [*quickly, walks to* KAREN]: What happened? [KAREN *shakes her head.*] What happened, Karen?

KAREN: He thought that we had been lovers.

MARTHA [*tensely*]: I don't believe you.

[*Wearily* KAREN *turns her head away.*]

KAREN: All right.

MARTHA [*automatically*]: I don't believe it. He's never said a word all these months, all during the trial—

[*Suddenly grabs* KAREN *by the shoulders, shakes her.*] Didn't you tell him? For God's sake, didn't you tell him it wasn't true?

KAREN: Yes.

MARTHA: He didn't believe you?

KAREN: I guess he believed me.

MARTHA [*angrily*]: Then what have you done?

KAREN: What had to be done.

MARTHA. It's all wrong. It's silly. He'll be back in a little while and you'll clear it all up— [*Realizes why that can't be, covers her mouth with her hand.*] Oh, God, I wanted that for you so much.

KAREN: Don't. I feel sick to my stomach.

MARTHA [*goes to couch opposite* KAREN, *puts her head in her arms*]: What's happened to us? What's really happened to us?

KAREN: I don't know. I want to be sleepy. I want to go to sleep.

MARTHA: Go back to Joe. He's strong; he'll understand. It's too much for you this way.

KAREN [*irritably*]: Stop talking about it. Let's pack and get out of here. Let's take the train in the morning.

MARTHA: The train to where?

KAREN: I don't know. Some place; any place.

MARTHA: A job? Money?

KAREN: In a big place we could get something to do.

MARTHA: They'd know about us. We've been famous.

KAREN: A small town, then.

MARTHA: They'd know more about us.

KAREN [*as a child would say it*]: Isn't there anywhere
to go?

MARTHA: No. There'll never be any place for us to go.
We're bad people. We'll sit. We'll be sitting the rest
of our lives wondering what's happened to us. You
think this scene is strange? Well, get used to it; we'll
be here for a long time. [*Suddenly pinches* KAREN *on
the arm.*] Let's pinch each other sometimes. We can
tell whether we're still living.

KAREN [*shivers, listlessly gets up, starts making a fire
in the fireplace*]: But this isn't a new sin they tell us
we've done. Other people aren't destroyed by it.

MARTHA: They are the people who believe in it, who
want it, who've chosen it. We aren't like that. We
don't love each other. [*Suddenly stops, crosses to
fireplace, stands looking abstractedly at* KAREN. *Speaks
casually.*] I don't love you. We've been very close to
each other, of course. I've loved you like a friend, the
way thousands of women feel about other women.

KAREN [*only half listening*]: The fire's nice.

MARTHA: Certainly that doesn't mean anything. There's
nothing wrong about that. It's perfectly natural that
I should be fond of you, that I should—

KAREN [*listlessly*]: Why are you saying all this to me?

MARTHA: Because I love you.

KAREN [*vaguely*]: Yes, of course.

MARTHA: I love you that way—maybe the way they said

I loved you. I don't know. [*Waits, gets no answer, kneels down next to* KAREN.] Listen to me!

KAREN: What?

MARTHA: *I have loved you the way they said.*

KAREN: You're crazy.

MARTHA: There's always been something wrong. Always—as long as I can remember. But I never knew it until all this happened.

KAREN [*for the first time looks up, horrified*]: Stop it!

MARTHA: You're afraid of hearing it; I'm more afraid than you.

KAREN [*puts her hands over her ears*]: I won't listen to you.

MARTHA: Take your hands down. [*Leans over, pulls* KAREN's *hands away.*] You've got to know it. I can't keep it any longer. I've got to tell you how guilty I am.

KAREN [*deliberately*]: You are guilty of nothing.

MARTHA: I've been telling myself that since the night we heard the child say it; I've been praying I could convince myself of it. I can't, I can't any longer. It's there. I don't know how, I don't know why. But I did love you. I do love you. I resented your marriage; maybe because I wanted you; maybe I wanted you all along; maybe I couldn't call it by a name; maybe it's been there ever since I first knew you,—

KAREN [*tensely*]: It's a lie. You're telling yourself a lie. We never thought of each other that way.

MARTHA [*bitterly*]: No, of course *you* didn't. But who says I didn't? I never felt that way about anybody but you. I've never loved a man— [*Stops. Softly.*] I never knew why before. Maybe it's that.

KAREN [*carefully*]: You are tired and sick.

MARTHA [*as though she were talking to herself*]: It's funny; it's all mixed up. There's something in you, and you don't know it and you don't do anything about it. Suddenly a child gets bored and lies—and there you are, seeing it for the first time. [*Closes her eyes.*] I don't know. It all seems to come back to *me*. In some way I've ruined your life. I've ruined my own. I didn't even *know*. [*Smiles.*] There's a big difference between us now, Karen. You feel sad and clean; I feel sad and dirty. [*Puts out her hand, touches* KAREN's *head.*] I can't stay with you any more, darling.

KAREN [*in a shaken, uncertain tone*]: All this isn't true. We'll pretend you never said it; you'll have forgotten it tomorrow.

MARTHA: Tomorrow? That's a funny word. In all those years to come, Karen, we would have had to invent a new language, as children do, without words like tomorrow.

KAREN [*crying*]: Go and lie down, Martha. You'll feel better.

MARTHA [*looks around the room, slowly, carefully. She is very quiet. Exits Right, stands at door for a second looking at* KAREN, *then slowly shuts the door behind her*]: Yes. I think I will feel better.

[KAREN *sits alone without moving. There is no sound in the house until, a few minutes after* MARTHA's *exit, a shot is heard. The sound of the shot should not be too loud or too strong; the act has not been sensational. For a few seconds after the noise has died out,* KAREN *does not move. Then, suddenly, she springs from the chair, crosses the room, pulls open door Right. Almost at the same moment footsteps are heard on the staircase.*]

MRS. MORTAR. What was that? Where is it? [*Enters door Center, frightened, aimlessly moving about.*] Karen! Martha! Where are you? I heard a shot. What was— [*Stops as she sees* KAREN *reappear Right. Walks toward her, still talking. Stops when she sees* KAREN's *face.*] What—what is it? [KAREN *moves her hands, shakes her head slightly, passes* MRS. MORTAR, *and goes toward window.* MRS. MORTAR *stares at her for a moment, rushes past her through door Right. Left alone,* KAREN *leans against the window.* MRS. MORTAR *re-enters crying. After a minute.*] What shall we do? What shall we do?

KAREN [*in a toneless voice*]: Nothing.

MRS. MORTAR: We've got to get a doctor—right away. [*Goes to phone, nervously, fumblingly starts to dial.*]

KAREN [*without turning*]: There isn't any use.

MRS. MORTAR: We've got to do something. Oh, its aw-

ful. Poor Martha. I don't know what we can do—
[*Puts phone down, collapses in chair, sobs quietly.*]
You think she's dea—

KAREN: Yes.

MRS. MORTAR: Poor, poor Martha. I can't realize it's
true. Oh, how could she—she was so—I don't know
what— [*Looks up, still crying, surprised.*] I'm—I'm
frightened.

KAREN: Don't cry.

MRS. MORTAR: I can't help it. How can I help it? [*Gradually the sobs cease, and she sits rocking herself.*] I'll
never forgive myself for the last words I said to her.
But I was good to her, Karen, and you know God will
excuse me for that once. I always tried to do everything I could. [*Suddenly.*] Suicide's a sin. [*No answer. Timidly.*] Shouldn't we call somebody to—

KAREN: In a little while.

MRS. MORTAR: She shouldn't have done it, she shouldn't
have done it. It was because of all this awful business.
She would have got a job and started all over again—
she was just worried and sick and—

KAREN: That isn't the reason she did it.

MRS. MORTAR: What—why—?

KAREN [*wearily*]: What difference does it make now?

MRS. MORTAR [*reproachfully*]: You're not crying.

KAREN: No.

MRS. MORTAR: What will happen to me? I haven't anything. Oh, she wouldn't have wanted me, no matter

what she said, to suffer and starve. I know she
wouldn't have wanted that.

KAREN: She was very good to you; she was good to us
all.

MRS. MORTAR: Oh, I know she was, Karen, and I was
good to her too. I did everything I could. I—I
haven't any place to go.

KAREN [*without malice*]: When the hawks descend, they
must be fed. You'll be taken care of.

MRS. MORTAR [*after a few seconds of silence*]: I'm afraid.
It seems so queer—in the next room. [*Shivers.*]

KAREN: Don't be afraid.

MRS. MORTAR: It's different for you. You're young.

KAREN: Not any more.

[*The sound of the door-bell ringing.* MRS. MORTAR
jumps. KAREN *doesn't move. It rings again.*]

MRS. MORTAR [*nervously*]: Who is it? [*The bell rings
again.*] Shall I answer it? [KAREN *shrugs.*] I think
we'd better. [*Exits down the hall through Center
doors. Returns in a minute followed by* MRS. TILFORD'S
maid, AGATHA, *who stands in the door.*] It's a woman.
[*No answer.*] It's a woman to see you, Karen. [*Getting no answer, she turns to* AGATHA.] You can't come
in now; we've had a—we've had trouble here.

AGATHA: Miss Karen, I've *got* to speak to you.

KAREN [*turns slowly, mechanically*]: Agatha.

AGATHA [*goes to* KAREN]: Please, Miss Karen. We've
tried so hard to get you. I been phoning all the time.

Please, please let her come in. Just for a minute, Miss Karen. Please—

MRS. MORTAR: Who wants to come in here?

AGATHA: Mrs. Tilford. [*Looks at* KAREN.] Don't you feel well? [KAREN *shakes her head.*] You ain't mad at *me*?

MRS. MORTAR: That woman can't come in here. She caused all—

KAREN: I'm not mad at you, Agatha.

AGATHA: Can I—can I get you something?

KAREN: No.

AGATHA: You poor child. You look like you got a pain somewhere. [*Hesitates, takes* KAREN'S *hands.*] I only came cause she's so bad off. She's got to see you, Miss Karen, she's just got to. She's been sittin' outside in the car, hoping you'd come out. She can't get Dr. Joe. He—he won't talk to her any more. I wouldn't a come—I always been on your side—but she's sick. If only you could see her, you'd let her come for just a minute.

KAREN: I couldn't do that, Agatha.

AGATHA: I don't blame you. But I had to tell you. She's old. It's going to kill her.

KAREN [*bitterly*]: Kill her? Where is Mrs. Tilford?

AGATHA: Outside.

KAREN: All right.

AGATHA [*presses* KAREN'S *arm*]: You always been a good girl. [*Hurriedly exits.*]

MRS. MORTAR: You going to allow that woman to come in here? With Martha lying there? How can you be so feelingless? [*She starts to cry.*] I won't stay and see it. I won't have anything to do with it. I'll never let that woman— [*Rushes sobbing from the room.*]

[*A second after,* MRS. TILFORD *appears in the doorway Center. She is a sick woman; an old woman. Her face, her walk, her voice have changed. She is feeble.*]

MRS. TILFORD: Karen, let me come in.

[*Without turning,* KAREN *bows her head.* MRS. TILFORD *enters, stands staring at the floor.*]

KAREN: Why have you come here?

MRS. TILFORD: I had to come. [*Stretches out her hand to* KAREN, *who does not turn. She drops her hand.*] I know now; I know it wasn't true.

KAREN: What?

MRS. TILFORD [*carefully*]: I know it wasn't true, Karen.

KAREN [*stares at her, shudders*]: You know it wasn't true? I don't care what you know. It doesn't matter any more. If that's what you had to say, you've said it. Go away.

MRS. TILFORD [*puts her hand to her throat*]: I've *got* to tell you.

KAREN: I don't want to hear you.

MRS. TILFORD: Last Tuesday Mrs. Wells found a bracelet in Rosalie's room. The bracelet had been hidden for several months. We found out that Rosalie had taken the bracelet from another girl, and that Mary

—[*Closes her eyes.*] that Mary knew that and used it to force Rosalie into saying that she had seen you and Miss Dobie together. I—I've talked to Mary. I've found out. [KAREN *suddenly begins to laugh, high and sharp.*] Don't do that, Karen. I have only a little more to say. I've talked to Judge Potter. He will make all arrangements. There will be a public apology and an explanation. The damage suit will be paid to you in full and—and any more that you will be kind enough to take from me. I—I must see that you won't suffer any more.

KAREN: We're not going to suffer any more. It's all too late. Martha is dead. [MRS. TILFORD *gasps, shakes her head as though to shake off the truth, feebly falls into a chair, and covers her face.* KAREN *watches her for a minute.*] So you've come here to relieve your conscience? Well, I won't be your confessor. It's choking you, is it? [*Violently.*] And you want to stop the choking, don't you? You've done a wrong and you have to right that wrong or you can't rest your head again. You want to be "just," don't you, and you wanted us to help you be just? You've come to the wrong place for help. You want to be a "good" woman again, don't you? [*Bitterly.*] Oh, I know. You told us that night you had to do what you did. Now you "have" to do this. A public apology and money paid, and you can sleep again and eat again. That done and there'll be peace for you. You're old, and the old are callous. Ten, fifteen years left for you. But what of me? It's a whole life for me. A whole God-damned life. [*Suddenly quiet, points to door Right.*] And what of her?

MRS. TILFORD [*she is crying*]: You are still living.

KAREN: And I don't know why.

MRS. TILFORD [*with a tremendous effort to control herself*]: I didn't come here to relieve myself. I swear to God I didn't. I came to try—to try anything. I knew there wasn't any relief for me, Karen, and that there never would be again. [*Tensely.*] But what I am or why I came doesn't matter. The only thing that matters is you and— You, now.

KAREN: There's nothing for me any more.

MRS. TILFORD: Oh, let's try to make something for you. You're young and I—I can help you.

KAREN [*smiles*]: You can help me?

MRS. TILFORD [*with great feeling*]: Take whatever I can give you. Take it for yourself and use it for yourself. It won't bring me peace, if that's what's worrying you. [*Smiles.*] Those ten or fifteen years you talk about! I hope it won't be that long. But however long it is, it will be in darkness. And I won't blame you if that gives you pleasure.

KAREN: It doesn't now. I'm too tired to want even that. [*Almost tenderly.*] You will have a hard time ahead, won't you?

MRS. TILFORD: Yes.

KAREN: Mary?

MRS. TILFORD: I don't know.

KAREN: You can send her away.

MRS. TILFORD: No. I could never do that. Whatever she does, it must be to me and no one else. She's—she's——

KAREN: Yes. Your very own, to live with the rest of your life. They will be years of darkness; you're right. [*For a moment she watches* MRS. TILFORD's *face.*] It's over for me now, but it will never end for you. She's harmed us both, but she's harmed you more, I guess. [*Sits down beside* MRS. TILFORD.] I'm sorry.

MRS. TILFORD [*clings to her*]: Then you'll try for yourself.

KAREN: All right.

MRS. TILFORD: You and Joe.

KAREN: No. We're not together anymore.

MRS. TILFORD [*looks up at her*]: Did I do that, too?

KAREN: I don't think anyone did anything, any more.

MRS. TILFORD [*makes a half-movement to rise*]: I'll go to him right away.

KAREN: No, it's better now the way it is.

MRS. TILFORD: But he must know what I know, Karen. You must go back to him.

KAREN [*smiles*]: No, not any more.

MRS. TILFORD: You must, you must— [*Sees her face, hesitates.*] Perhaps later, Karen?

KAREN: Perhaps.

MRS. TILFORD [*after a moment in which they both sit silent*]: Come away from here now, Karen. [KAREN *shakes her head.*] You can't stay with— [*Moves her hand toward door Right.*]

KAREN: When she is buried, then I will go.

MRS. TILFORD: You'll be all right?

KAREN: I'll be all right, I suppose. Good-by, now.

[*They both rise.* MRS. TILFORD *speaks, pleadingly.*]

MRS. TILFORD: You'll let me help you? You'll let me try?

KAREN: Yes, if it will make you feel better.

MRS. TILFORD [*timidly*]: And you—you'll take the money?

KAREN [*tired*]: If you want it that way.

MRS. TILFORD [*with great feeling*]: Oh yes, oh yes, Karen.

[*Unconsciously* KAREN *begins to walk toward the window.*]

KAREN [*suddenly*]: Is it nice out?

MRS. TILFORD: It's been cold. [KAREN *opens the window slightly, sits on the ledge.* MRS. TILFORD *with surprise*] It seems a little warmer, now.

KAREN: It feels very good.

[*They smile at each other.*]

MRS. TILFORD: You'll write me some time?

KAREN: If I ever have anything to say. Good-by, now.

MRS. TILFORD: You will have. I know it. Good-by, my
dear.

[KAREN *smiles, shakes her head as* MRS. TILFORD *exits.
She does not turn, but a minute later she raises her
hand.*]

KAREN: Good-by.

CURTAIN

Printed in the United States
85371LV00004B/287/A